Transforming School Leadership With ISLLC and ELCC

Neil J. Shipman
University of North Carolina
Chapel Hill

J. Allen Queen
The University of North Carolina
Charlotte

Henry A. Peel
East Carolina University

EYE ON EDUCATION
6 DEPOT WAY WEST, SUITE 106
LARCHMONT, NY 10538
(914) 833–0551
(914) 833–0761 fax
www.eyeoneducation.com

Library of Congress Cataloging-in-Publication Data

Shipman, Neil J.
   Transforming school leadership with ISLLC and ELCC / Neil J. Shipman,
J. Allen Queen, Henry A. Peel.
          p. cm.
ISBN 1-59667-034-7
    1. School principals--United States. 2. Educational leadership--United
States. 3. Education--Standards--United States. I. Queen, J. Allen. II. Peel,
Henry A. III. Interstate School Leaders Licensure Consortium. IV. Title.
LB2831.92.S534 2007
371.2'012--dc22   2006102571

10 9 8 7 6 5 4 3 2 1

Editorial and production services provided by
Rick Soldin, Electronic Publishing Services, Inc.
172 Harmony Farms Drive, Jonesborough, TN, 37659
423-348-7333   www.epsinc-tn.com

Also Available From Eye On Education

School Leader Internship: Developing, Monitoring, and Evaluating Your Leadership Experience, 2nd Ed.
Martin, Wright, Danzig, Flanary, and Brown

The Instructional Leader's Guide to Informal Classroom Observations
Sally J. Zepeda

**Lead with Me:
A Principal's Guide to Teacher Leadership**
Gayle Moller and Anita Pankake

**Countdown to the Principalship:
A Resource Guide for Beginning Principals**
O'Rourke, Provenzano, Bellamy and Ballek

Data Analysis for Continuous School Improvement
Victoria L. Bernhardt

**The Administrator's Guide to
School Community Relations, Second Edition**
George E. Pawlas

**The Principal's Purpose:
A Practical Guide to Moral and Ethical School Leadership**
Leanna Stohr Isaacson

**Smart, Fast, Efficient:
The New Principals' Guide to Success**
Leanna Stohr Isaacson

**The Principal as Instructional Leader:
A Handbook for Supervisors**
Sally J. Zepeda

Instructional Leadership for School Improvement
Sally J. Zepeda

Supervision Across the Content Areas
Sally J. Zepeda and R. Stewart Mayers

**What Great Principals Do Differently:
15 Things That Matter Most**
Todd Whitaker

Comments from the Field

"The book is a benchmark volume in the struggle to help school leaders learn to lead for student success and rates as an exemplary and unrivaled narrative in the quest to anchor leadership education on the ISLLC and ELCC Standards."

Joseph Murphy
Professor of Public Policy and Education
Peabody College of Education
Vanderbilt University

"Shipman and colleagues have written a very practical guide for those who wish to strengthen the preparation of educational leaders. The standards for educational leadership, developed by outstanding scholars and practitioners, represent a state-of-the-art consensus on research and the wisdom of practice that should be used to design programs to prepare the next generation of leaders. Such programs will prepare leaders who can create and sustain environments that will support student learning in today's standards-based educational world."

Arthur E. Wise, President
National Council for
Accreditation of Teacher Education

"*Transforming School Leadership* by Shipman, Queen and Peel provide an invaluable toolkit to help both principals and those responsible for their development. It brings the ISLLC and ELCC standards to life through citations of good research and through thoughtful, practical advice. Those who lead schools, or who aspire to lead, have a clear pathway to creating the schools America needs."

Joseph S. Villani
Deputy Executive Director
National School Boards Association

"Leadership in schools is more complex than ever before—it's also more rewarding! Henry Peel, Allen Queen, and Neil Shipman have captured the essence of the challenges and the rewards. This book provides essential insights into the practice of school leadership and does so within the context of the most highly regarded professional standards. Simply put, this book is a must for leadership preparation programs and any practitioner's professional library."

Dr. Michael Ward
Superintendent (Retired), North Carolina
Department of Public Instruction
Professor, University of Southern Mississippi
Department of Educational Leadership

Contents

The ISLLC and ELCC Standards

To download the the ISLLC and ELCC Standards, please visit these web pages:

ISLLC – http://www.ccsso.org/content/pdfs/isllcstd.pdf

ELCC – http://www.npbea.org/ELCC/ELCCStandards%20_5-02.pdf

Acknowledgements

The authors would like to personally thank all of the M.S.A. students at the University of North Carolina at Chapel Hill, the University of North Carolina at Charlotte and East Carolina University for their assistance in the development of this book. We are also most appreciative to practicing principals, superintendents and other central office personnel (some who were our doctoral students) who provided input and offered suggestions for improvement throughout the entire process.

Our special thanks go to Stanley A. Schainker for permitting us to include several of his wonderful case studies and to some of the true giants in the field including Joseph Murphy, Arthur Wise, Robert Cole and Michael Ward who read our work and offered wonderful words of support. Thank you.

Finally, we would like to thank our publisher, Bob Sickles for his patience, support and trust in this project and to his editorial staff who put the final touches to the book. Thank you, Renae Szad for your marathon session checking references.

Meet the Authors

Dr. Neil J. Shipman was the first Director of the Interstate School Leaders Licensure Consortium (ISLLC) and is now an educational consultant and Clinical Associate Professor in the Department of Leadership at the University of North Carolina at Chapel Hill. Prior to that, Dr. Shipman had served a large and diverse suburban school system as a Principal, Supervisor of Instruction, an Area Director for Instruction, and as Acting Associate Superintendent. His publications and presentations focus on the principal's role in improving instruction, professional development for school leaders, and the impact of the ISLLC Standards on the education reform movement. Dr. Shipman has been instrumental in affecting program reform in higher education, which he believes to be his greatest professional achievement.

Dr. J. Allen Queen is currently a professor and former Chair of the Department of Educational Leadership at the University of North Carolina at Charlotte. He has been a classroom teacher, principal, college administrator, and a consultant to over 300 school districts and professional organizations in 45 states and 5 foreign countries. His work focuses on block scheduling, responsible classroom management and school discipline, student transitions, and professional time and stress management. Dr. Queen has written 36 books, over 100 professional articles, and has appeared on numerous radio and television programs, including *ABC World News*.

Dr. Henry A. Peel, Vice Provost at East Carolina University in Greenville, North Carolina, also holds an endowed chair in the Department of Educational Leadership as the Wachovia Distinguished Professor. Before joining the Department of Educational Leadership, he served in numerous leadership positions in the North Carolina public schools. He has written 11 books and book chapters and 39 journal articles and published proceedings. He is a frequent presenter at regional, national, and international conferences.

Introduction to the ISLLC and ELCC Standards

A New Vision of School Leadership

Educators and policy makers, as well as parents and community and business leaders, agree that we urgently need school leaders who can lead students to success in school. More importantly, we need school leaders with the capacity and foresight to usher students, teachers, and communities into the 21st century of education. Over the past decade, school reformers have pushed for the establishment of effective performance standards designed to measure the success of school leaders and strengthen educational leadership as a whole.

Foremost among the initiatives earning state and national support is the Interstate School Leaders Licensure Consortium (ISLLC), initially a collaboration of 24 state educational agencies and 11 professional development organizations committed to raising performance standards for school leaders. Since its inception in 1995, the ISLLC has established rigorous standards that establish performance goals for effective leadership, along with knowledge, disposition, and performance indicators to help define each standard. The combined experience of the members of the Consortium, coupled with research linking educational leadership and productive schools, underpinned the creation of the ISLLC *Standards for School Leaders* (Council of Chief State School Officers 1996).

The ISLLC (2002) maintains that school leadership roles require professional practice driven by criteria and standards focused on the development of effective leadership. School leaders need grounding in the knowledge and understanding required of an instructional leader and a lifelong learner. In establishing the Standards, the Consortium aimed to reform the concepts of educational leaders and raise the bar for school leaders to enter and stay in the profession. The ISLLC Standards present a comprehensive set of guiding principles for administrators in the 21st century. At this printing, 43 of the states' department of public instruction that license or certify school principals now use the ISSLC Standards.

A New Focus for Preparing School Leaders

The job description and responsibilities of principals have changed dramatically in the past 50 years. In the past, school administrators were viewed as managers, primarily concerned with efficiently running a school. Like leaders of typical bureaucratic organizations, principals ran schools with information, rules, policies, and procedures emanating from the top and working downward. The school's instructional program was essentially concerned with teaching children the basics. Therefore, educational programs that prepared school administrators looked quite different from the ones of today. Just as principals' roles have evolved in response to the intricate webs of educational reform, the standards used to evaluate educational leadership programs have undergone substantial redesign.

The current standards, similar to the ISLLC Standards, used to assess principal preparation programs are the Educational Leadership Constituent Council (ELCC) Standards, developed for the National Council for Accreditation of Teacher Education (NCATE) under the auspices of the National Policy Board for Educational Administration (NPBEA).

National Policy Board for Educational Administration Members

American Association of Colleges for Teacher Education (AACTE)
American Association of School Administrators (AASA)
Association for Supervision and Curriculum Development (ASCD)
Council of Chief State School Officers (CCSSO)
National Association of Elementary School Principals (NAESP)
National Association of Secondary School Principals (NASSP)
National Council for Accreditation of Teacher Education (NCATE)
National Council of Professors of Educational Administration (NCPEA)
National School Boards Association (NSBA)
University Council for Educational Administration (UCEA)

Educational Leadership Constituent Council Members

American Association of School Administrators (AASA)
Association for Supervision and Curriculum Development (ASCD)
National Association of Elementary School Principals (NAESP)
National Association of Secondary School Principals (NASSP)

First published in 1995 as *Guidelines for Advanced Programs in Educational Leadership*, the ELCC Standards aimed to help current and future school administrators meet the changing demands of society and schooling.

Within five years after publication of the ELCC Guidelines, NCATE changed its approach to assessing teacher education programs. Rather than focusing on the contents of a program's syllabi, the criteria address "how well graduates are prepared to perform in the workplace" (NPBEA 2002, p. 6). During the same period, the hallmark ISLLC Standards (1996) took hold in many states.

In response to these developments, NPBEA and NCATE agreed to revise the Guidelines to integrate them within the widely used ISLLC framework and to reflect changes in the NCATE approach. NPBEA convened a design team composed of faculty and school practitioners and chaired by Scott Thomson, past NPBEA executive secretary. After extensive review and adjustment, the working group presented the revised ELCC Standards to NCATE in 2001 (NPBEA 2002).

According to former NPBEA Executive Secretary Joe Schneider (2002), "These new standards will enable institutions of higher education to revise their graduate programs in educational leadership to ensure that their graduates have the knowledge and skills necessary to provide quality leadership for schools and school districts. . . . The standards strongly suggest that universities and colleges prepare administrators who are, first and foremost, concerned with improving teaching and learning." Schneider concludes with the directive that "we're expecting institutions of higher education to prepare educational leaders, and the emphasis is on instructional leadership."

Programs and departments of educational administration or educational leadership desiring NCATE accreditation are now required to meet the ELCC Standards as part of the institutional review. Those administrator-training programs that satisfy the Standards receive "national recognition" by NCATE and NPBEA (2002).

Assumptions Underlying the ELCC Standards

Several assumptions guided the development of the new Standards. These assumptions included the belief that

1. The central responsibility of leadership is to improve teaching and learning.
2. The purpose of the Standards is to improve the performance of school leaders, thereby enhancing the performance of teachers and students in the workplace.
3. The Standards apply to the most common positions in educational leadership, including principal, supervisor, curriculum director, and

superintendent but specifically exclude business managers. While the emphasis in preparation programs may shift among the standards depending upon specific leadership roles (i.e., potential superintendents may focus more on finance and policy development, while potential principals may focus more on instructional programs and student personnel), it is important for all school leaders to be familiar with and able to accomplish the tasks associated with each standard as well as to participate in an extensive internship.

4. The exercise of leadership in its various expressions constitutes the core function of principals, curriculum directors, supervisors, and superintendents. Leadership is active, not passive. It is collaborative and inclusive, not exclusive. While leadership may be viewed as a process, it also requires the exercise of certain expertise and the expression of particular attributes.

5. No overarching theory of leadership has proven adequate, but many of the skills and attributes of effective leadership are understood and can be taught and practiced.

6. Preparation programs should focus primarily on developing school leaders for responsible positions in elementary and secondary schools. This preparation requires the cultivation of professional competence through bridging experiences and clinical practice as well as classroom performance activities.

7. Many preparation programs fall short of developing the knowledge, skills, and attributes required of school leaders in today's workplace. Principals, curriculum directors, supervisors, and superintendents need increasingly to take initiative and manage change. They must build a group vision, develop quality educational programs, provide a positive instructional environment, apply evaluation processes, analyze data and interpret results, and maximize human and physical resources. They also must generate public support, engage various constituencies, and mitigate value conflicts and political pressures. School leaders clearly must be prepared to operate in the community as well as in the academy.

8. Leadership includes an ethical dimension because principals and other leaders are moral agents responsible for the welfare and development of students. Preparation programs should provide opportunities for candidates to formulate and examine an ethical platform upon which to rely when making tough decisions.

9. Preparation programs should be essentially an institutional responsibility, but the design and delivery of these programs should include

participants from school districts. In addition, some key learning experiences must take place in operating schools, particularly the application of knowledge and the practice of skills.

10. The standards should be assessed primarily through performance measures. Increasingly, schools are responding successfully to performance-based criteria and educational leadership preparation programs can benefit from similar processes. This approach provides a useful review of contemporary practice and the rationale for that practice.

(NPBEA 2002, 8–9)

While there are no clear and absolute best models in the literature of how to best prepare school principals, -researchers at Stanford University are leading a major study in the attempt to find the best model to be used. In the *School Leadership Study: Developing Successful Principals* (2005), the researchers, (Davis, Darling-Hammond, LaPointe and Meyerson) in their review of literature listed four "key findings" in their search: essential elements of good leadership, features of effective programs, multiple pathways to leadership development and policy reform and finances. In their analysis, the researchers acknowledged the impact that the principal has on student achievement, but more research is needed in some areas including curriculum and adapting to "local contexts". Evidence was presented that imply a strong relationship among some components such as being research-based, use of cohorts and having curricular coherence. Several models of program-based programs were presented and could be labeled as: university school districts, third party (nonprofits and statewide leadership academies) and partnership programs. The SLS, as it has become known, is in the process of examining "eight highly developed pre-and in-service program models that address key issues in developing strong leaders. (Davis et al. 2005).

From a slightly different perspective, researchers at the Southern Regional Education Board (SREB) in Atlanta, in their August 2006 report, "Schools Can't Wait: Accelerating the Redesign of University Preparation Programs," summarized their findings in four major conclusions.

1. Current state policies and strategies intended to promote redesign of principal preparation programs have produced episodic change in a few institutions but have fallen short in producing the deep change that would ensure all candidates master the knowledge and skills needed to be effective school leaders today.

2. There is a lack of urgency for refocusing the design, content, process and outcomes of principal preparation programs based on the needs of

schools and student achievement and little will happen until there are committed leaders of change at every level—state, university, and local school districts.

3. States and districts cannot depend on universities to change principal preparation programs on their own because the barriers to change within these organizations are too deeply entrenched.

4. The issue is not whether principal preparation programs need to change, but how states can plan and carry out a redesign initiative that gets the right results (Spence 2006).

The call by Spence and the SREB for immediate action appears to be addressed to the states' leadership, the governors and state legislators. Spence in his opening comments of the report, states that, "the commitment of governors and state legislators to make the preparation of quality school leaders a state priority is essential—as is united leadership from higher education, and K through 12 leaders at the state and local levels." (Spence, 2006). It is of great interest to the authors that the SREB in this document, delineate a clear set of four core conditions for the process of redesigning principal programs once states have take appropriate action as suggested above. These four cores are as follows:

Core Condition One: University/district partnerships for principal preparation.

Core Condition Two: Emphasis on knowledge and skills for improving schools and raising test scores.

Core Condition Three: Well-planned and supported field experiences.

Core Condition Four: Rigorous evaluation of participants' mastery of essential competencies and program quality and effectiveness.

(2006 SREB)

The authors hope that both of these fine organizations continue their research. Joining the debate about which model may be the best approach to use is not our intention or the purpose in this book. We simply share the latest thinking and concerns about developing the best models possible for preparing future principals to lead our nation's schools and applaud all efforts and intentions with this goal in mind.

In is our strong position as former principals, university administrators, and professors and our lead author, Neil Shipman, the former Director of ISLLC, that the ISLLC and ELCC Standards will provide the guidance necessary for any model, if implemented completely and accurately, to be the best program possible. These Standards have sustained for several years now and are still firm in their intent. There is little argument, if any, that these Standards can lead the way to the desired success in whatever capsule or format selected such as a traditional university program, to a program that is individualized, self-paced, module-based, and computerized, and anything in between. Our additional focus and readdress of some of the broad intentions of the Standards will further each candidate's probability of success. The detailed activities, Major Class Activities, case studies, and discussion approaches will further enhance a broad array of learners, from the beginning graduate student or teacher entering an academy to a seasoned, practicing principal working in the school. There is something for everyone to learn.

We believe that colleges/universities, school academies, or a well-planned university/school partnership can utilize these Standards with the approaches we suggest to ensure that their programs prepare principals to be effective school leaders. Each chapter in the book correlates with the corresponding Standards by number. In the remaining chapters of this book, we present what we call the essential knowledge for the prospective principal preparing for the profession and the essential elements for practice embedded in the ISLLC and ELCC standards. Specific questions and activities and a major class activity are at the end of each chapter, focusing on particular issues within the standards facing the principal today and tomorrow. Suggested readings are listed after each chapter and the references cited are listed at the end of the book.

Suggested Readings

Murphy, J. (ed.). 2002b. *The Educational Leadership Challenge: Redefining Leadership for the 21st Century [101st Yearbook of the National Society for the Study of Education]*. Chicago: National Society for the Study of Education.

Murphy, J., J. Yff, and N. Shipman. 2000. Implementation of the interstate school leaders' licensure consortium standards. *International Journal of Leadership in Education 3*(1), 17–39.

Levine, A. (2005). Educating school leaders. Washington, DC: The Education Schools Project.

Davis, S., L. Darling-Hammond, M. LaPointe, and D. Meyerson, 2005. *School Leadership Study: Developing Successful Principals* (Review of Research). Stanford, CA: Stanford University, Stanford Educational Leadership Institute.

1

Standard One:
Vision as an Essential of
Leadership Development

A leader is the person you would follow to a place you wouldn't go by yourself.

—Joel A. Barker

ISLLC Standard 1	ELCC Standard 1
A school administrator is an educational leader who promotes the success of all students by facilitating the development, articulation, implementation, and stewardship of a vision of learning that is shared and supported by the school community.	*Candidates who complete the program are educational leaders who have the knowledge and ability to promote the success of all students by facilitating the development, articulation, implementation, and stewardship of a school or district vision of learning supported by the school community.*

In this chapter, we will discuss a number of issues related to creating a vision for the school or district. As described in ISLLC Standard 1 and ELCC Standard 1, a successful school leader must have the knowledge and ability to develop and articulate a vision for success of all students. In this chapter, we explore the means for developing a vision and then discuss articulating and implementing the vision over time. As is the structure in each chapter, since the ELCC Standards were developed using the ISLLC framework, we give the ISLLC Standard along with the ELCC Standard.

At the start of this chapter, we present a number of terms pulled directly from the knowledge, dispositions, and performances associated with ISLLC Standard 1. The intent is to give a brief explanation of each term to set the stage for this chapter and then move to in-depth information related to the essentials of leadership for the ELCC Standard. We close with a look at visionary leadership.

Essential Knowledge for School Leaders

Under the knowledge, disposition, and performance indicators described in this ISLLC standard, leaders should be knowledgeable in the following areas: pluralistic society, strategic plans, systems theory, data collection and analysis strategies, communication skills, consensus-building skills, negotiation skills, vision, high standards of learning, continuous improvement, self-reflection, and organizational accountability.

Pluralistic society. Banks and Banks (2006) contend that "the mastery of basic skills will be essential but not sufficient as the diversity within our society deepens and our nation faces new challenges and possibilities." As principals lead schools today, it is increasingly important to recognize that all students are being prepared to meet the national and global needs for the 21st century. Principals must assist teachers to create an inclusive environment by incorporating diversity issues and promoting the democratic ideals of this nation. Schools must help students acquire the knowledge needed to construct civic, moral, and just communities that promote the common good. In the current push for quality, high-stakes testing, and accountability, it is essential that the principal recognize the need to discuss equity and justice as well.

"Maintaining a democratic society and preserving and enlarging freedom require citizens who embrace democratic values and recognize their responsibility to help narrow the gap between real and idealized American values" (Banks and Banks, 2006). Principals must participate actively in creating schools that equip students with these attitudes and skills.

It is imperative that principals consider their role in leading schools in a pluralistic society. It is not enough to simply say *All children can learn.* Principals must create learning communities in which the faculty and staff continue to examine ways to meet the needs of all children. The school's foundation of social justice and equity should be apparent throughout the school building, the curriculum, and the strategic directions of the school.

Strategic planning. A principal as a strategic planner is a recently embraced expectation that has been stressed in the last decade of school leadership. In many cases, strategic planning comes down to compiling an unwieldy (albeit comprehensive) document that takes a great deal of time to produce but is rarely used. It is time for principals to improve this process.

While strategic planning in schools is often too cumbersome, reflecting on what is being done and where the school is going is a very good practice. What we suggest changing is the accumulation of the multinotebook strategic plan. Instead, create with the faculty, staff, and other stakeholders a few focused strategic directions. These directions may have short- or long-term timelines and should be used to direct and establish a framework for decisions in leading the school. This approach offers a living process that is more viable, easy to adjust, and easier to use.

According to the Public Education Network (2001, p. 1), "Strategic planning is a formal and systematic process of focus, assessment, issue identification, and strategy development." We have identified six basic steps in a comprehensive strategic planning process:

1. Developing a common vision.
2. Identifying goals.
3. Setting priorities.
4. Developing programs and budget requirements.
5. Implementing programs.
6. Annually evaluating progress in attaining the identified goals.

Developing a common vision is the critical first step. Much will be written in this chapter to help readers with the process. The vision is the guide on which all decisions for the school should be made. School leaders should constantly and consistently ask, "How does this help us to fulfill our vision?"

We recommend that a strategic plan, while being kept concise, should be designed for a five- to six-year implementation process. Involvement of all affected stakeholder groups, both internal and external to the school, is crucial. Time spent carefully and thoroughly identifying these key groups prior to actual development of a strategic plan will help to assure acceptance of the final product.

Be wary of producing long lists of goals and objectives followed by even longer lists of strategies to accomplish them. Identify a few crucial issues. Ask what would happen to the school or district if an issue is not addressed, and if the answer is, "Nothing," that issue should not be part of the strategic plan. To be useful, the document must be concise, easy to read, and user friendly. Detailed plans can be developed by those persons responsible for implementation and do not need to be part of the strategic plan itself.

During the implementation phase, be consistent in referring groups and individuals back to the vision, mission, and goals. Always ask how an idea, request, or suggested change will help to attain the vision, accomplish the mission, or meet a specific goal.

Following development of several specific goals, form action-planning teams for each goal. These teams should develop general strategies and plans. Concurrently, a financial advisory committee should be working to identify areas in the strategic plan that will require additional resources and determine how those resources could be generated.

Prior to acceptance by local school groups or by a district board of education, several public forums should be conducted to gather input and obtain ownership. Such forums could be scattered throughout different phases of the development process.

Systems theory. For preparation in this area, principals should consider reviewing educational systems. Understanding the school as an interactive system—determining its components, how they relate and interact, and how the parts are dependent upon each other—is crucial to creating efficient systems. According to Beckhard and Pritchard (1992), a major part of systems thinking is looking for connections in the system. The principal should know how changes in one part of the system might affect other parts of the system. This does not mean creating elaborate and complex school improvement models, but setting clear directions for improvement while recognizing that making a change in one part of the system impacts the other. Changing something as simple as student traffic flow can affect the instructional program, for example. That is, routing students to lunch a certain way can minimize interruptions to instructional time for other students—or if the change is not thought through, it can have the opposite effect.

Data collection and analysis strategies. A school vision appropriately centers on student success in schools. As a part of the new accountability, the analysis of that success must be data driven. Federal- and state-funded projects often require documented evidence that school programs lead to verifiable improvements in student achievement; furthermore, citizens and policy makers expect schools to justify the value and effectiveness of their programs. Also, educators have come to recognize that they can no longer rely on "intuition, tradition, or convenience" in setting directions and making decisions about instructional strategies. Instead, educators have embraced the idea that collecting and analyzing data is the key in justifying and verifying improvements in student achievement. The principal has an important role in guiding data-driven reform processes. In fact, data analysis must be the basis for sound educational decision making. By systematically collecting and analyzing data and, most importantly, distributing data to teachers, you can assist teachers in determining strengths and weaknesses in student knowledge and skills. These data provide meaningful guidance in adjusting instructional practices (Wade 2001).

Data analysis should be used to identify gaps in achievement as well as to determine the effectiveness of specific programs. This need not involve statistical analysis. Useful data analysis can be done in two basic steps—collecting the data and then using it to develop and attain instructional improvement goals (Creighton 2001). From a wider perspective, data gives a clear profile of the entire school and can be used to determine how the school compares to others in the district and often the state, region, and nation. Most importantly, accepted by a faculty, educators can use this data to the formulation and implementation of corrective courses of action that can solve problems and assist the faculty in meeting a school's goals. It is suggested that the principal take a proactive role in data collection and analysis. In this era of accountability, the essential role of the principal is guiding a data-driven school improvement process. As Creighton implied that using data to make instructional leadership decisions in a new way of thinking.

Communication skills. More than ever, principals must be adept at communication. First of all, you must be able to clearly articulate the vision and direction of the school. It is important to make the community aware of the purpose of the school and its practices and programs. In essence, you are marketing the school to the community.

Next, principals must be able to effectively interact on a daily basis both in writing and orally. Lehr (2001) suggests that good writing by school administrators depends on a clear sense of audience and purpose and that they should view their writing as exemplifying the high expectations of student writing. Make each memo or letter a carefully constructed communication that effectively delivers the intended message. Write all forms of written communication at an appropriate level for the audience you are addressing—always avoiding jargon. A principal cannot be careful enough in written communication. Be as concise as possible, but say enough to make the point clear. Determine when it is best to create a written response versus communicating orally—if the written response seems too complicated, it probably is. Create good, consistent formats when writing memos, letters, and other documents that can continue to improve over time.

Understanding how to deal with the media is a critical skill for school leaders to master. In today's society, the public receives its information primarily from the Internet and television. These two sources provide most of what is believed. Computers have changed communications to be instantaneous, available worldwide, and instigated by anyone who has access to the technology.

School leaders have more control over information sharing than most realize. Provide information to the media in a manner they can use. For example, reporters like sound bites: short, colorful, quotable statements. Use visuals as backdrops and props whenever possible. Television and computers are visual tools, as are pictures and diagrams in print media. What the audience sees may often be as important as what is said, and making yourself understood matters more than presenting a long list of statistics. Always remember your audience. Who will be watching, reading, or listening to what you have to say? What will make them sit up and say "Aha!"?

On television and in the newspapers, your physical appearance makes a difference to your credibility. If you have advance notice of contact with a media person, professional dress is the order of the day. The small frame of a television set distorts the way people look, so smile; make eye contact with the reporter; have good but relaxed posture; stand still; show animation with positive head and facial movements; don't shout, don't whisper, and speak a little more slowly than usual. Be conscious that 60 percent of what the audience will remember is the visual image; 30 percent is how it sounds (funny, sad, serious); and 10 percent is what is actually said.

There are several types of interviews in which a school leader may participate:

◆ *Local news programs.* The interviewee will be given an average of 100 seconds, including 12 to 15 seconds of sound bites. A feature will be about two and a half minutes and a segment is five to six minutes. Try to make two or three points and be consistent in staying with those points.

◆ *Public affairs programs.* Watched by legislators, regulators, policy makers, other media people, and community leaders, these shows are usually done on Sundays, a traditionally slow news day. However, the audience members are generally extremely influential.

◆ *Radio.* Most likely, a school leader's time on radio will be on one of the very popular talk shows. In this format, have a lot to talk about so there is not a lot of quiet time when the host can be talking or asking questions. Dead air time also gives more time for disaffected callers to call in to ask often pointless and negative questions.

◆ *Print.* Print reporters tend to be assigned specifically to education issues, so they will be more knowledgeable in that area and will spend more time with you. (This also indicates that on TV, the school leader is the expert.) Again, use only two to three major points, and try to restrict your discussion to those key points.

Always go into any interview with a very clear set of objectives and three talking points. Be prepared to take control, stay on the offensive, and be able to dominate the conversation. Phrase answers to questions in complete sentences that can stand alone. Keep in mind that questions on a television interview are rarely heard or seen—just the respondent's answer. Try not to deny the negative, but respond with a positive statement. Never be defensive.

Be systematic in preparing. Try to identify the problem or topic ahead of the interview. What are some of the major issues that might be covered in an interview at this particular time of the school year? Who are the key people involved in the issue at hand? What are the consequences for the decision or action taken? How can you ensure that people will pay attention to your side of the discussion? If you have time to plan ahead by writing down what you want to say, you may be able to relate your three points to any question in some manner. Focus on what you are going to say, not what the reporter is going to ask. Do not say too much.

The following are several "message enhancers" that can be used to strengthen an interview response:

- Specific examples.
- One-liners (sound bites).
- Quotes from the experts or the opposition.
- Data—proportions that people can understand (nine out of ten, two thirds, 96 percent, etc.).
- Absolutes.
- High-impact and colorful words.
- Personal experiences and anecdotes.
- Analogies.
- A second-person perspective (what your message means to your audience).

David Kushma, former editor of the Memphis *Commercial Appeal*, suggests several media commandments for school leaders (personal communication, 2000):

- Do not lie. You *will* get caught. When you do, 'fess up and apologize. The public is generally forgiving.
- Do not talk "off the record." There is no such thing.
- Spend as much time as needed explaining a situation. If you don't know the answer, say so, but offer to get back to the reporter by the deadline.
- Don't argue. Don't give "cutesy" answers.
- Listen very carefully to what is being asked. Stay focused.
- Do not blame the central office, but do help the audience understand their position. Don't pass the buck. Don't give your personal opinion. You are not the judge or jury.
- Build trust. Your reputation is more powerful than the media's. (One way to do this is to invite local education reporters to the school for personal meetings with you.)

Neil Offen (personal communication, 2004), editor of the Chapel Hill, North Carolina *Herald,* says, "The worst time to meet a reporter for the first time is during a crisis. . . . We are not the enemy."

Consensus-building skills. Having strong communication skills is critical to facilitating consensus building. While consensus building allows a healthy debate of the pros and cons of a particular issue, it depends on an atmosphere of trust so that participants feel they can express ideas without fear of ridicule. You should encourage—and reward—such risk taking.

To build consensus, the principal must facilitate the flow of conversation so that it moves forward, by restating, clarifying, and engineering the group to an end point. It may be impossible to get 100 percent agreement, but ask participants if they can at least live with—that is, support and implement—the decision. Unlike decisions made by majority rule, which may leave up to half of the group unwilling to support the outcome, decisions by consensus should reduce the likelihood of sabotage. You may need to reassure participants that if things need to be revisited, the floor is open for discussions at a later time. That is, "Since we can all live with this solution, let's all give it our best shot. As we implement, if you see problems, bring them back to the group for resolution—don't just go your own way or blame others." We will return to the topic of consensus building later in this chapter.

Negotiation skills. The skills needed to be effective at negotiation are similar to those for consensus building. We suggest using negotiation when there is a conflict of interest or differing views in which the parties involved prefer to search for a solution instead of giving in or simply walking away with no resolution. The principal can work with both parties to see if there is a reasonable resolution in which each side feels that some of their needs are met while possibly giving in on less important items.

A critical part of negotiating, as in most communication, is listening. What is it that this person or group really wants? Next, the principal must determine what items are negotiable and nonnegotiable. It is important to know what is in your span of control and what leverage you feel you have. Remember that equity is an important part of making these decisions—would the same concessions be made for someone else asking for the same consideration?

Vision. Much of this chapter focuses on vision and its importance to the principal. Since we discuss the topic at length below, we will treat it only briefly here. Simply stated, the vision is the description of an organization when the organization is at its peak performance. That is, the vision describes what the organization should look like. It should be clearly stated and easily understood. It may entail elements that currently exist as well as elements for which the organization strives. Much more attention will be given to the entire area and related elements of vision later in the chapter.

High standards of learning. In establishing high standards for students, the principal should gather input from teachers, central administration, parents, and the community. These standards can support higher levels of learning if directly aligned to specific goals worthy of effective instruction and promote teaching responsive students learning styles. Additional, education can use standards to keep students and parents apprised of progress, to diagnose special support for students, and to evaluate school practices (Fall 2002).

Continuous improvement. Creating a continuous improvement model for the school is a mind-set that allows the principal to assess current successes and needs, build on the successes, and work to improve the areas of need. It says that the school leadership is continually checking systems, making adjustments, and striving to do better. Much has been written about Deming's concept of continuous improvement. This concept may be defined as stabilizing the process through identification and resolution of problems, making active improvements as are necessary, and monitoring and maintaining the process (Neave 1990). There are a number of approaches to implementing a continuous improvement model, but simply stated, it can be defined as constantly asking, "What can I do even better? How can I do this or that even better?" Challenge yourself with these questions, but also ask the entire school faculty and staff to do the same.

Self-reflection. When reflecting on ones actions self reflection is a crucial action in supporting future actions. Many higher-education preparation programs strive to produce "reflective practitioners" (Sheerer 2003). These are educators who reflect on their actions, their theories and beliefs, and their assumptions about their role as an educator. As a leader, it is important to continually practice self-reflection and ask yourself why you respond in a certain way, why you react to certain stimuli, what knowledge you have that will help you resolve a situation, and so on. According to Dewey (1933), reflection "involves active, persistent, and careful consideration of any belief or supposed form of knowledge in light of the grounds that support it and the further consequences to which it leads." We suggest that as principal, you should create time for reflection—you'll have to carve it out of a busy schedule—and use it to refine your leadership skills. Many principals find it useful to keep a reflection journal for this purpose.

Organizational accountability. High-stakes testing and accountability programs will become even more prevalent in this next decade. Federal legislation will push states to create new systems or modify current standards to ensure that their educational guidelines are met. Principals will be charged with defending their schools' success with concrete defensible data. We recommend that you adopt a proactive posture to your organization's accountability. Be aware of needed improvements and be able to clearly articulate what your school is doing to address these areas. Be equally aware of your school's success and use it to market your school.

The effectiveness of a school can be described by either the characteristics of the school or the leadership attributes of the principal. According to the Connecticut School Effectiveness Project, an effective school has seven characteristics (Lunenburg and Ornstein 2000):

1. A safe and orderly environment for teachers and students
2. A clear school mission
3. A principal who is an instructional leader
4. A climate of high expectations for students
5. A high time-on-task learning environment
6. A program of frequent monitoring of student progress
7. A positive home–school relationship with strong parent support

Role of the Principal in Building a Vision

Authors of current literature depict the administrator as the keeper of the dream. The school leader is the creator of the dream and the driving force that moves the dream forward. The role of the administrator is to manage the vision of the school. The role of the school leader is to establish visionary leadership. Leaders initiate visionary leadership with an image of the organization for the future, shared among stakeholders to grant empowerment and gain ownership and acceptance of a unified vision. Effective leaders inspire stakeholders, direct the path to success, and assist the organization in dealing with change.

Murphy (1994) determined "vision-building activities have direct effects on teacher's personal goals" as cited in (Murphy and Louis 1994). Therefore, school leaders must utilize vision as a tool to influence personal teaching improvement goals and reflect commonalities embraced by all. Murphy and Louis also identified teachers' perceptions of school goals and school culture as two conditions directly affecting teacher commitment.

School leaders must master an understanding of school culture to alter perceptions of school goals. Teacher perceptions of school goals ultimately determine the degree to which teachers seek ownership of shared values within the school. "A school's culture is a complex pattern of norms, attitudes, beliefs, behaviors, values, ceremonies, traditions, and myths that are deeply ingrained in the very core of the organization" (Barth 2002). In addition to understanding the implications of school culture, principals must create a climate and culture for successful change. The school leader, modeling the vision of success, enhances a culture for change. The principal plays a significant role in setting the school climate for students and teachers. Making clear the behavioral expectations for students and dealing with them in a fair manner is essential. A caring environment can be created through daily conversations with students. School leaders must communicate enthusiastically about the vision, encourage risk taking, and celebrate success while upholding high expectations for school improvement in the midst of failures and constant change.

School leaders can emerge from any level of the organization, but, ultimately, the vision is the school principal's responsibility. An effective educational leader uses the shared vision to work with all stakeholders and accomplish goals for improved student achievement.

The principal will lead teachers through a collaborative process of "identifying the type of learning experiences (curriculum and instruction) that will be used to implement the vision." Effective leaders provide stakeholders with opportunities for collaborative work to "select or develop curricula, instructional materials, and assessment measures that are consistent with the view of learning as expressed in the vision statement." Keepers of the vision facilitate community and school partnerships to develop a community engagement program. Effective educational leaders "develop a set of evaluative indicators that will be used to measure progress toward the stakeholders' vision and to develop a means of reporting that progress to the stakeholders of the school district" (Wallace, Engel, and Mooney 1997, p. 12).

Principals remain the facilitators of the shared vision throughout the process of gaining and continuing the commitment of a new vision. According to Lashway (1997), "creating readiness is crucial."

School leaders must provide teachers opportunities to analyze and reflect on the school's current culture. Teachers must examine current beliefs, develop a rationale for change, and consider new models and strategies for school improvement. Schools having successfully restructured a vision and analyzed data supporting assumptions assist study groups in understanding the current state of the organization and the need for change (Lashway 1997).

The authors believe that to institutionalize the vision is critical and regardless of how beautifully the document is written, it must be concrete and direct the stakeholder to follow policies programs and procedures. The school leader must be the guide. How do leaders facilitate vision?

To sustain credibility, the school leader must embed the vision in the curriculum, staffing, evaluation, and budget. The vision lacks credibility and becomes a stagnant document failing to serve the intended purpose without full ownership from all stakeholders.

School leaders must remain focused on the intentions of the vision for the classroom. Teachers directed by awareness and enthusiasm do not necessarily see the implications of the vision for teaching (Elmore, Peterson, and McCarthy 1996). Elmore found that teachers have great difficulty internalizing the systematic knowledge to demonstrate a practice ensuring the vision becomes reality. To remedy the inability to embed the vision into daily practices, principals must provide teachers with continuous assessment, analysis, and professional development to overcome the barriers of conceptualizing the vision.

The school leader must ensure that the vision exists as a cyclical process. The learning community works collaboratively to create a vision and implement, articulate, and revise based on experiences and new knowledge. Principals must work in joint effort with stakeholders to review values and reflect on the vision's influence or the core activity of schools—teaching and learning. Along with developing a learning community, the educational leader must provide time, data, and resources for stakeholders to examine school policies and practices ensuring alignment of instructional practices with the school vision.

Essential Elements for School Leaders

ELCC Standard 1: Candidates who complete the program are educational leaders who have the knowledge and ability to promote the success of all students by facilitating the development, articulation, implementation, and stewardship of a school or district vision of learning supported by the school community.

To rise above mediocrity, any organization or leader must have a vision. Thomas Jefferson had a vision; we call it the Declaration of Independence. Martin Luther King, Jr., had a dream that was his vision. When Senator Robert Kennedy quoted George Bernard Shaw —"Some people see things as they are and say, why? I see things as they could be and say, why not?"—he demonstrated his vision.

Nanus (1992) viewed vision as a directional sign post for others to follow while Hughes, Norris, and Ubben (2001) defined vision of a combination of three main actions: creation, communication, and steadfast commitment providing important direction from a broader perspective.

Be wary of confusing vision with mission and goals. A mission is like the road map to a destination, with goals as specific targets to help the organization get there. A vision is much broader, grander in its intent. It may even be something we ourselves cannot reach in our tenure at a school. It will take diverse groups of people and, most likely, succeeding groups working on the goals to eventually reach the vision.

Loeb and Kindel (1999) define vision as an overarching idea or a doable dream, while a mission is a statement that summarizes goals to fulfill the vision, and goals are intermediate steps that when attained contribute to accomplishing the mission.

Without a vision, the mission and goals, no matter how worthwhile, lose coherence. Without a clear and shared sense of purpose, school programs become fragmented, teachers lose motivation to try new techniques and to push for higher standards for students, work in general becomes dissipated and undirected, and curricula and general instruction suffer.

With a vision, the mission and goals become powerful guides. Organizational vision allows an organization to achieve more than the sum of its parts. Eventually, the impossible becomes possible. The dream becomes reality.

Recently, a panel of outstanding school superintendents was asked to name the most important characteristics they seek in hiring principals for their districts. Each superintendent looked for a principal who is first and foremost a visionary leader—that is, a leader able to develop a vision and then articulate, implement, and promote the vision. It is not surprising that both the ISLLC and ELCC designate vision as their first standard.

Developing a Vision

While it is not difficult to accept the rationale for *having* a vision, it is more difficult as a leader to actually be charged with developing a vision. One reason is that the leader cannot establish the direction alone; the school must create a vision that states what the school believes (Ubben, Hughes, and Norris 2001).

The first important step to developing a vision is to understand that it must be a living direction that is visited each day. Too often, leaders feel that a vision is a direction statement established in a meeting at the beginning of the school year just to meet the requirements of school planning—a statement that, once written, is never used. A *living vision* provides a focus that engenders strategic directions for leading the organization.

To create the living vision, the principal must involve all stakeholders in the development process. This makes each stakeholder group more vested in the success of the organization. This highly interactive process may take a bit of time, but that is time well spent. After working with many organizations to assist them in creating a vision, we recommend the following steps:

- *The principal determines the nonnegotiables*—what must be a part of the vision for the school to succeed. For example, you must ensure that the vision focuses on promoting success of all students. It may not be necessary to express these nonnegotiables, as they may emerge naturally. If they do not, you should bring them forward for discussion. Also, while you should have ideas of how the school should improve, you must also remain flexible on negotiable items to ensure that the voices of the stakeholders are heard throughout the process.

- *The principal develops an open process.* You should allow input from the various stakeholders. For example, you may call together the faculty and staff and invite them to describe what the school would look like if it were doing its very best, or ask them to do so individually. After all, that is the vision—the description of the school if it were doing exactly what it should be doing. For example: *This is a school where every child experiences success every day.*

- *The principal guides consensus building.* While 100 percent agreement is unlikely, you should work for consensus on the living vision. The process should involve representatives of all aspects of the school community. This accomplishes a vision that is broad based and comprehensive. It also creates ownership for the vision and a working knowledge among the many school community groups of the direction the school needs to move. Though often time-consuming, the process is worthwhile. A vision statement is the overall belief that the stakeholders agree upon. It is a representation of the school's needs as well as the educational philosophies of the school's community members (Ubben, Hughes, and Norris 2001).

According to F. P. Schargel (1994), the development of the mission statement is important in aligning the members of the organization to their common vision. This is a crucial step because it provides a direction for the school and creates a cooperative force within the school's stakeholders. A goal moves the school forward, but it may not ever be totally achieved (Ubben, Hughes, and Norris 2001).

Burt Nanus (1992) has identified several characteristics of powerful and transforming visions:

- They are appropriate both for the organization and for the time at hand.
- They set standards of excellence and reflect high ideals.
- They clarify purpose and direction.
- They inspire enthusiasm and encourage commitment.
- They are well articulated and easily understood.
- They reflect the uniqueness of their organization and what will make it special.
- They are ambitious and expand the organization's horizons.

Graduate students in a master of school administration program at the University of North Carolina at Chapel Hill have identified several additional characteristics of effective visions:

- Positive
- Communicated often
- Reflecting community values
- Concise
- Flexible
- Developed collaboratively
- Inclusive
- Focus on student achievement
- Understandable by all
- No jargon

Much has been written on the subjects of vision, leadership, and visionary leadership. In order to develop a vision, a leader must know his or her organization, involve critical individuals, explore all possibilities, and with the organization put the vision down in writing (Mendez-Morse et al. 2001).

According to the United States Charter Schools organization, the vision should embrace five fundamental aspects: "values, educational approach, curriculum focus, customer focus, and outcomes and goals" (USCS 2004, p. 2).

The North Central Regional Educational Laboratory describes visioning this way: "To choose a direction, a leader must first have developed a mental image of a possible and desirable future state of the organization. This image, which we call a vision, may be as vague as a dream or as precise as a goal or mission statement. The critical point is that vision articulates a view of a realistic, credible, and attractive future for the organization, a condition that is better in some important ways than what now exists" (NCREL 2002).

Articulating a Vision

A crucial part of the leader's job is to communicate the vision as valued and achievable. Through your actions and words, you present its components to the faculty and staff, parents, students, and community members. Remember, your school community has created a living vision—one that you will articulate daily, reminding all stakeholders of the direction the organization has committed to taking.

This living vision influences decisions concerning all aspects of educating students, including budget decisions, personnel decisions, and instructional decisions. It is also a valuable tool for assessing proposed programs and activities. Ask yourself, "Is this aligned with the organization's vision?" If the answer is "yes," you can proceed with a realistic decision-making process. If the answer is "no," you can articulate to the stakeholders why the proposal is not appropriate.

Implementing a Vision

A visionary leader must also do the following: attract commitment and energize people, create meaning in workers' lives, establish a standard of excellence, bridge the present to the future, and transcend the status quo. When the participants accept a common vision, it is then possible to begin moving toward the attainment of that vision (NCREL 2002). Implementing a vision can be defined as "asking questions about what might be, standing for something, making certain others know what that 'something' is, and determining appropriate courses of action for getting to expressed goals" (Hughes et al. 2001).

"Vision seems to distinguish leaders from those who are simply good managers" (Ubben, Hughes, and Norris 2001). A school and a school district should be defined by this vision, and it should permeate all aspects of change and operations in the school and in the district.

A vision statement does not suffice as school improvement. You must turn it into action and make it part of the school culture. As you move forward, do not lose sight of the big picture, and do not allow minor setbacks and obstacles to hinder attainment of the vision. Do all you can to make those who created the vision excited and eager to attain it.

Implementation Plan

There are four basic steps involved in implementing a school vision (Mendez-Morse et al. 2001). These steps are general, and there is room for modification. As a future or beginning principle, what changes would you make?

- *Know the organization.* Focus on what people pay attention to. A principal must know the needs, faults, weaknesses, and strengths of the school. "Knowing what a school or district is about and the reason for its existence is the first step in developing a vision statement. Knowing the collective understanding of an organization is the second step and includes participation of constituencies."

- *Involve critical individuals.* This involvement will negate the criticism that may come later with dissatisfaction among the critics. The addition of outside opinions may help to bring a different perspective to the discussion as well. The saying "keep your friends close and your enemies closer" comes to mind.

- *Explore the possibilities.* Consider future plans for growth, assignment boundaries, end-of-course test scores, and current areas that need improvement in the school. Specific questions: What are possible trends of future needs? What are future societal expectations or requirements?

- *Put it in writing.* People are more likely to do things that are written down. The statement should be submitted to final review by faculty and staff and then committed to paper to become a reality.

Stewarding a Vision

The role we see as the instructional leader and the one with a task of selling and providing guidance in attaining a vision. Just as you must embody the qualities you seek in the faculty and staff as well as in the students, so you must model the behaviors that will lead to realization of the school vision. Students and teachers determine what you value by observing what you pay attention to.

Do not hesitate to modify and fine-tune the vision. Representatives from all stakeholder groups must revisit it annually. Keep it a living vision—if it is too rigid, frustration will set in. School populations and issues change, and so should the vision statement of the school.

It is the role of the principal to facilitate the creation, implementation, and constant reinforcement of the vision statement. A vision statement gives current employees direction when making decisions, offers future employees a perspective on what the school is about, and enables future students to determine the priorities of the school.

Visionary Leadership

In 1990 Grady and Lasourd concluded that there were five qualities dominant in visionary leaders. Visionary leaders are motivated by personal values, strongly committed to the achievement of goals, organized innovators, believers in shared decision making, and consistent projectors of a future that represents a better tomorrow for the organization (Broadway and Smith 1997).

In response to the societal demands affecting the educational realm in the past decade, the school administrator must become a leader of change. Schools exhibit change "in response to various pressures, including parental complaints about the quality of education, labor market demands for increasingly skilled workers, rapid advances in technology, and the growing popularity of public school alternatives. . . ." School administrators are no longer resource and task managers. With student achievement at the forefront of the educational arena, school administrators direct more focus toward "teacher and student learning, professional development, data-driven decision making, and accountability" (Institute of Educational Leadership 2002) in efforts to maximize individual student success.

McCay (2001) believes content knowledge is inadequate for social change and school reform initiatives and acknowledges the importance of recognizing and nourishing school principals through opportunities to learn, reflect, and change. Despite limited time, school leaders require opportunities to focus on personal learning. Principals gain firsthand knowledge of best practices and programs through hands-on learning, facilitating meaningful feedback, and welcoming an array of new ideas to strengthen leadership skills and techniques. Leaders seek interaction with colleagues from different school districts to provide meaningful feedback as well as an array of new ideas for strengthening leadership skills and techniques. Just as students benefit from the opportunity to reflect on learning experiences, principals require adequate time to examine assumptions, assess situations, and analyze problem-solving strategies.

King (2002) identifies several responsibilities of the school leader's role that go beyond that of serving as a learning leader. Principals must develop leadership capacity and skills to effectively implement data-based decision-making, analyze data, and share results among stakeholders. Establishing a learning community begins with creating conditions for professional development. A professional learning community is "an environment that fosters mutual cooperation, emotional support, and personal growth as educators work together to achieve what they cannot accomplish alone" (King 2002).

Principals of the 21st century must employ leadership roles defined in terms of instructional leadership, community leadership, and visionary leadership. While striving to reach ongoing objectives such as creating a mission, setting and implementing school-wide goals, enhancing the learning community, or assisting as instructional leader, principals must display visionary leadership. Visionary leadership not only "demonstrates energy, commitment, entrepreneurial spirit, values, and conviction that all children will learn at high levels, but also inspires others with the vision both inside and outside of the school building" (Institute for Educational Leadership 2000).

Vision is a futuristic element bringing forth the skills, talents, and resources necessary to make the vision a reality. To ensure stakeholder ownership, the vision must be realistic, credible, and attractive, a natural extension of the organization. Stakeholders award credibility when they believe the vision is realistic. The vision is considered influential as stakeholders gain interest in and demonstrate commitment to the vision.

Leaders must establish a personal vision prior to leading an organization. Effective visionary leaders do not impose personal visions upon stakeholders. By examining personal beliefs, values, and goals, leaders formulate a personal belief system and guide the development and commitment of a shared vision.

Stakeholders exhibiting a wealth of imagery project a clear picture of the future. "By providing a picture, vision not only describes an organization's direction or goal but also the means of accomplishing it" (Hord 1992). Creators of the vision should specify descriptive and precise goals to clarify individual roles in the transformation to success. The vision should "speak to the quality of human relations and the competencies and attributes that learners will carry away from the learning environment. Vision is a goal oriented belief that individuals are willing to strive for in order to attain the ideal state. . . . The vision statement for a school is the basis for an action plan to develop and implement an agenda to put the vision of excellence into practice" (Wallace 1997). To expand upon the vision, stakeholders create goals for achievement of realistic vision. How the principal attains this reality is the essence of visionary educational visionary leadership.

Suggested Readings

Data Based Decision Making National Association of Elementary School Principals (NAESP)Virginia: Author.

Starratt, Robert J. 1995. *Leaders with Vision: The Quest for School Renewal*. Thousand Oaks, CA: Corwin Press.

Suggested Activities

1. Complete a brief reflection about the material in Standard 1 in your reflection journal.

2. Using the case study *The Case of Mountville High by Dr. Shipman* (on page 21), write a brief concept paper describing how you would use the major concepts in this chapter as the newly appointed principal of Mountville High School. (This activity could also be a small-group cooperative project by completing the activities within and at the end of the case study.

3. In small groups, use Nanus's seven characteristics of powerful and transforming visions to critique four real vision statements found through the Internet or from a school you know. Each group should select one vision as an exemplar and be able to defend the selection based on Nanus's characteristics. The groups should also be able to describe why the other three visions were not selected as exemplars.

4. Select one of the two books from the suggested readings for Chapter 1 to read and critique. Prepare a brief paper (four to five pages) that includes an overview, information about the authors, and the book's value to a school leader.

5. *For Class Practice:*
   Divide into representative groups as the various stakeholders. While the process can take many forms, we describe here one model for facilitating the discussion. Begin with each stakeholder writing an individual vision statement, and then ask individuals to collaborate in small groups to assess the statements and write a consensus statement on which all agree. Finally, invite one group to share their vision with the entire assembly as a starting point. Other groups can identify similarities with their own consensus statement. As you facilitate the discussion, allow each group to add aspects not yet included.

The outcome is the first draft of a vision that includes direction from all stakeholders. Have the entire group review the draft to ensure that all the necessary areas and directions are included. Disregard grammar and readability at this point—spend time on the aspects of the vision. A subcommittee can perform final wordsmithing and clarifying once the group has approved the draft.

MAJOR CLASS ASSIGNMENT:
Vision and Standard 1

The Futurists

In the 1990s there were discussions about revisiting the concepts of the school philosophy known as futurism. Educational thinkers through history have been interested in the influence of the school upon the future. However, only recently has a group of thinkers known as futurists made an impact upon educational policy and practice. Similarly to the radicals, futurists wished to fully reform education, yet they tend to take a less radical approach. They see the history of education in this country as a basis to build on, but also a foundation to learn from. They agree with the radicals that a total transformation is necessary, that mere improvement of our educational system will not suffice (Schlechty 1990). For them, however, the task is to transform—and yet preserve—the purpose of education.

Future students will still need to know the basics of reading, writing, and arithmetic; they will still need to learn about and understand the American culture and political system; and they will still need to have marketable skills. However, they must also learn how to continue to acquire and apply knowledge in the future; they must learn to become lifelong learners and thinkers, because "in the information society, knowledge and the ability to use it are power" (Schlechty 1990, p. 40). For them, the task of schools now is to rethink their purpose and better prepare students for the fast-paced, ever-changing world of Alvin Toffler's *Future Shock* and *The Third Wave* and the person of tomorrow must be intellectually and emotionally capable of living in a strange new world (Myers and Myers 1995).

While understanding the past, controlling the present, and shaping the future are aims expressed by both pragmatists and social reconstructionists, futurists move beyond this position to argue for another proposition—namely, that the person of tomorrow must be intellectually and emotionally capable of living in a strange new world, which will require adaptation and survival skills.

Some futurists stipulate that schools should constitute and promote participatory democracy both through what they teach and by their example as operating institutions. Rather than prepare students for a past that no longer exists or a present that is rapidly disappearing, teachers should, by their teaching and their example, prepare students to live in democracy with many unknowns. Students, in order to live satisfactorily in this future, must acquire strategies for adaptation and survival. Adaptation, in particular, will require that students learn to think for themselves. Independent thought by the adult of tomorrow involves, among other abilities, thinking ethically and creatively.

According to most futurists, the school that cultivates independent thinking should also stimulate autonomous decision making. More than ever before, the future will belong to people who think and choose for themselves. This aim, developing tomorrow's thinkers and choosers, is partly an outcome of schooling that attempts to produce both liberally educated people and highly trained specialists. It advances along with students who recognize both the autonomy and the responsibility implied by the concepts of studying and learning. Students who learn to think independently, live democratically, choose ethically, interact tolerantly, and act wisely offer hope and promise for the future (Myers and Myers 1995).

The Case of Mountainville High School: Survival or Demise?

Congratulations. You have recently been appointed as the new principal of Mountainville High School, from which you graduated only a short 15 years ago. At the time you graduated, Mountainville High was the premier school in Lakem County, with an enrollment of 1357 students in grades 7 through 12. Previously widely recognized as a school of excellence, Mountainville now has an enrollment of 654 students in grades 7 through 12 and is projected to have less than 500 students within three years. Traditionally, the dropout rate in this school has been well below the state average, and more students went on to four-year colleges proportionately than in any high school in the state. When there were over 1300 students there was a wide variety of extracurricular offerings both in sports and in nonathletic activities. As the enrollment has declined, so too has the ability to offer a wide variety of extracurricular activities. However, the smaller school size is exciting to you, as you have recently received a master's degree in school administration from Waukama State and are very aware of the many advantages of small high schools.

Only three years ago, seniors at Mountainville scored the fifth highest of any high school in the state on the new state exit exam. Since then, there has been a precipitous drop in test scores, enough for a takeover by the state. The county's two elementary schools are presently averaging an enrollment in K through 6 of 448 students each. So far, their scores remain in the average range except for the 28 percent who are Native Americans. These two schools are 52 miles from one another. Mountainville High is geographically closer to a neighboring county than it is to the elementary feeder school that is farthest away (73 miles).

Built in 1960 as a state-of-the-art high school facility, the physical plant, while architecturally still pleasing as a landmark in the community, is badly in need of repairs and renovations. The state department of education facilities office has estimated it would cost over $10 million to bring this building up to minimal 21st-century standards.

Although rural geographically, when you were growing up in this county, the taxable base was considered to be affluent due to the successful textile mills within its boundaries. When outsourcing to other countries began to occur and the mills quickly closed, the tax support for schools entered a period of steep and rapid decline. Concurrent with this fiscal decline was a decline in county population, with nearly 50 percent of the population relocating to urban areas about 200 miles from this district. Data indicate that the majority of the citizens who relocated were between the ages of 25 and 50, thus causing a concomitant decline in school enrollment. Slowdown County has been able to maintain a reasonable tax base since there are several megafarms owned by large conglomerates within its borders. In fact, they just opened a new $28.5 million high school.

Parents love the smallness and personalization of Mountainville High, but are beginning to voice concerns about whether or not their children will be able to find well-paying work and/or attend a quality college when potential employers and admissions officers review the school's accountability reports. Ninety-seven percent of the parents of students in the school also graduated from the school. Many of them were in school at the same time as you, and are welcoming you back after teaching for ten years in the big city. They just know you will understand their problems and concerns. Max Richman, your best friend in high school, is now president of the local bank and chair of the county commissioners. There have been a few rumors circulating that you were brought back from the big city to either close the high school or, at the very least, consolidate with the new high school in Slowdown. Max has been reassuring people that you are "too nice a guy" to do that. He also reminds you often who your kin are. While *site-based management* is not a formal term in the district, parents are very used to being major players in school decisions, even though there is no longer an official local board of education due to the state takeover. The existing board is advisory until the state deems it appropriate to return control to them.

Your teaching staff is very experienced, having an average tenure of 20.6 years in the district. Of the 30 teachers in the school, their experience times range from 2 years to 36 years. Four of them have master's degrees, and two are not yet on tenure. The average salary is $38,250. As far as you can determine, at least six teachers are teaching out-of-field. These data have serious implications for meeting the demands of "highly qualified" teachers as defined in the No Child Left Behind Act of 2001. All but eight of the teachers grew up in Mountainville High. Three of the most experienced are related to you, including your Aunt Kathryn. Most of them were your teachers when you were a student at Mountainville.

Four of your teachers double as bus drivers and thus start their day at 6 A.M. and finish their last run after 6 P.M. Many of the students are so tired when they arrive at the school in the morning after a one- to two-hour bus ride that they fall asleep in the earliest class periods. Others are unable to stay for after-school activities because they have no way to get home except on the school bus, and there is no funding for an activity bus. You read in a recent American Association of School Administrators journal that more than 100 rural districts in the United States have moved to a four-day workweek. This is an extremely interesting concept to you. On the other hand, you think to yourself, if the kids are tired in a five-day week, how would they cope with a longer school day in a four-day week? This concept will need a lot of study before it moves toward fruition.

You will personally need to teach calculus to the college-bound juniors and/ or seniors, as you have been unable to find a teacher willing to come to Mountainville who is qualified to teach calculus. The only foreign language offered is Spanish, and there is some question about whether the teacher is competent enough to go beyond the first two years of this language. The last advanced placement (AP) course stopped being offered two years ago when Jim Thomas, the AP history teacher, moved to another state. Since there is only one qualified teacher in chemistry and physics, these subjects must be taught in alternate years. Block scheduling was considered last year as a possible solution to this problem, but the veteran teachers strongly resisted it and convinced your predecessor that it is just another one of those newfangled big-city notions.

Technology as you were accustomed to it in the city district is very limited in this rural community. Although the figures are very rough estimates from the central office, it appears as though fewer than 25 percent of the families enrolled in the school have computers at home. There is one small computer lab in the school with 15 seven-year-old computers. The local telephone company has donated free dial-up service to the Internet for a single line in the school. *Distance learning* is a brand-new term for your veteran teachers as well as most parents and students. No professional associated with the school district seems to have ever heard of "e-rate."

Although there is a central office, in reality it is of little use. There is no longer a superintendent, so the director of curriculum is nominally in charge of day-to-day operations for the three schools in the district. She has one secretary, who handles all fiscal issues, and two professional staff, one who is your immediate supervisor, and one who handles all district noninstructional issues. The noninstructional supervisor has recently informed you that the district could save $496,000 if they just did not have that high school. Two of the three central office professionals have each been in the system for 29 years, and this is the twenty-third year for the curriculum director. The secretary has been there for 35 years, starting when her father was the superintendent of schools. None of these four can believe the changes that are occurring in this place they have called home for more than 55 years each. When assistance is needed for any situation beyond their capacity, they call on the state department staff or neighboring Slowdown County.

Of course, rarely do they face any problems they can't solve themselves. They remain oblivious to the pending lawsuit threatened by the county's three doctors regarding lack of medical supervision at athletic events at Mountainview.

Appointed by the state board of education due to the state's takeover of the district last year, you have been charged with either bringing the test scores back to the preeminence of ten years ago or developing a consolidation plan with Newton High School in the adjoining Slowdown County. They have not ruled out major construction to modernize the building, but have indicated that state construction funds are very limited.

Your first task is to develop a tactical plan for these alternative goals, including a timeline. You will report directly to the state superintendent of schools, who has been charged by the state board with oversight responsibilities for the Lakem County district. The tactical plan is due to the state superintendent by January 31 of this school year.

Suggested Student Assignments/Tasks

For all assignments the student is expected to note to which ISLLC and ELCC Standards the response most closely relates and why. Major concepts from this text that are utilized in your responses should be specifically noted.

1. Knowing the myriad problems facing the school leader of Mountainville High School, develop a rationale based on dispositions that would explain why anyone would want to be its principal.

2. Based on the information stated and implied in this case study, identify several goals for yourself as principal as well as for the school and broader community.

3. Provide a draft of the tactical plan you will present to the state superintendent of schools and explain the process you will use to develop this plan.

4. In small groups, brainstorm lists of advantages and disadvantages of rural schools as described in the case study. Follow this with members of the group taking parts of your lists to find support in the literature for the items in your lists.

5. Will site-based management as a governance tool for this school be an asset or detriment? What does the research say to support your position?

6. This school has a different kind of "minority achievement gap" than most educators are used to discussing. How will you, as the school leader, eliminate this gap, or should this not be a priority until the other issues are resolved? If the latter, how would you explain this to the 28 percent of your families who are Native Americans?

7. How will you work with concerned community members who want Mountainville High kept open, no matter what the stated negative consequences are, especially when they remind you that this school's academic achievements

have been consistently better than those in Slowdown County? Remember as you develop this plan that you may also have to deal with the citizens of Slowdown, if it is determined that consolidation may be a viable option.

8. What, indeed, are the options available to this principal to solve all the problems of Mountainville High? Provide theoretical and research support for each solution you suggest. Are your solutions proactive or reactive; traditional or nontraditional; risk aversive or risk taking? Why?

9. What are the major policy and political issues related to each of your proposed solutions? Describe the strategies the principal could use to positively address these policy and political issues.

10. Which of the problems at Mountainville High School could also be problems in a suburban or an urban school district? If this principal and school were faced with such similar problems in a suburban district, what strategies would need to be different and why? In an urban setting?

2

Standard Two: Instructional Culture as an Essential of Leadership Development

The principal is the head learner, engaging in, displaying, and modeling the behavior we expect and hope teachers and students will adopt.

—Roland Barth

ISLLC Standard 2	ELCC Standard 2
A school administrator is an educational leader who promotes the success of all students by advocating, nurturing, and sustaining a school culture and instructional program conducive to student learning and staff professional growth.	*Candidates who complete the program are educational leaders who have the knowledge and ability to promote the success of all students by promoting a positive school culture, providing an effective instructional program, applying best practice to student learning, and designing comprehensive professional growth plans for staff.*

ELLC Standard 2 deals with creating a school culture conducive to student learning. The Standard's emphasis on relevance, engagement, responsibility, dignity, diversity, empowerment, participation, and praise mirrors the effort to find more successful ways to respond to ever-increasing societal challenges brought to public schools. Under the knowledge, disposition, and performance indicators described in this ISLLC Standard, leaders should be knowledgeable in the following areas: student growth and development; learning theories; motivational theories; curriculum design, implementation, evaluation, and refinement; principles of effective instruction; measurement, evaluation, and assessment strategies; diversity; adult learning principles; professional development models; change process; technology; professional growth; management functions; school cultures; and student learning.

Essential Knowledge for School Leaders

Student growth and development. Student academic achievement is the focus of schools. However, recent shifts in perspective require school leaders to respond with methods emphasizing student growth and development at their foundation. Student or learner-centered curricula are focused on student outcomes. Instruction includes the interactive engagement of teacher with students, and students to and with other students in an exchange of behaviors that include but are not limited to discussions, lectures, debates, games, and simulations. Robert Sylwester, in *A Celebration of Neurons: An Educator's Guide to the Human Brain* (Alexandria, VA: Association for Supervision and Curriculum Development, 1995), reviews brain theory and research and makes a strong case that students are more apt to learn and connect to the material they are being taught in school if their emotions are engaged (Hinebauch 2000). School leaders, with the ability to develop school environments capable of meeting the developmental needs of students, increase the likelihood of success for all students, but especially for those who are considered at risk of meeting the needs of the 21st-century student.

Learning theories. Theories of learning tend to explain, describe, or predict the various components included in the process as to the relationships of each component to one another. Theories of learning encompass the assumptions and beliefs about how children develop, what they should be learning, and what kind of outcomes they need to achieve. As a principal, you should have a basic understanding of major learning theories and their impact on student learning and development. Three of the major learning theories you should be familiar with are the behaviorist theory of learning, the cognitive theory of learning, and the constructivist theory of learning.

Basically, behaviorism, whose major 20th-century proponent was psychologist B. F. Skinner, is based on a behavior-reward system that reinforces correct behavior. A key element in behaviorism is immediate feedback about the behavior. Cognitivist theory is based on the idea that learning is based on making symbolic, mental constructions involving active mental processing on the part of the individual learner. While behaviorism is focused on observable behavior, cognitive learning is more interested in the process of how one thinks about something. Constructivist theories of learning propose that children "construct" their knowledge through personal experiences. This knowledge is internalized and made a part of their schemata, or cognitive history.

Motivational theories. Motivational theory to some imply that motivation is not a single dimensional construct, but rather it is situational or dependent. School leaders must sort through many theories of motivation and the forces affecting individuals and schools. Awareness of the broad range of approaches can help school leaders recognize effective methods.

Examination of motivational theories such as attribution, goal determination, and self-determination are useful entry points for school leaders. Understanding the reasons students give for success or failure is important to understanding how the school environment may unknowingly be communicating messages about student ability. There is general consensus that motivation is an internal state or condition that can serve as a catalyst to activate, thereby giving one direction, but the debate continues.

Curriculum design, implementation, evaluation and refinement. Curriculum has been conceptualized as a planned course of action for intended learning outcomes, while instruction has been referred to as an entity dealing with how a proposed curriculum is put into action. Consequently, teachers were viewed as implementers in their classrooms of externally created curricula and instructional materials that were prescribed for them.

One view describes designing curriculum as similar to giving students maps helping them to successfully navigate the path of learning (Schultz and Delisle 1997). Curriculum also is described as a tool for appropriately placing the resources of teaching and learning. Resources are distributed by determined norms or values, which can be stated or simply understood. The former view requires school leaders to be travelers with students and teachers. Developing a sense of the route to be traveled is valuable to school leaders. Developing an understanding of the values influencing views and actions of students, teachers, and the community can help school leaders maximize available resources and positively impact student learning.

Curriculum designs include universal models, which implies the development of instructional materials and activities that allow learning goals to be attainable by individuals with wide differences in their abilities to see, hear, speak, move, read, write, understand English, attend, organize, engage, and remember (Orkwis 1999).

School leaders have many strategies at their disposal in their approach to refining curricula. Reeve describes curriculum as a strategy that takes course content and shapes it into an effective plan for teaching and learning (Reeve 2002). Developing, implementing, and evaluating curricula through a planned approach focuses refinement efforts and assists school leaders in meeting the teaching and learning needs of schools.

Principles of effective instruction. Definitions of effective instruction must include the evaluation of each aspect of school impacting student achievement. School leaders are responsible for decisions that extend beyond the doors of the school to the individual student in the classroom.

Effective educators must make decisions based on accurate information. School leaders of today must be able to evaluate the effectiveness of decisions in diverse areas such as individual learning styles, professional development, data analysis, community involvement, and management of the organization and facilities. Issues of community and self-efficacy are especially important when school leaders are evaluating the effect of instruction targeted to at-risk students (Royal and Rossi). Connecting interpersonal relationships to efforts to improve the effectiveness of instruction in schools is necessary if the efforts are not to be overcome in a firestorm of resistance and anger (Royal and Rossi 1997). Effective instructional leaders with a positive impact on student learning frequently talk with teachers and promote professional development. Learning, understanding, and using these types of behaviors must be included in the skills school leaders acquire in achieving the goal of effective instruction.

Program evaluation strategies. Measurement must go beyond the testing of students academically. Data-driven decision making requires that school leaders seek out, interpret, and act on information gathered. Methods used need to provide decision makers with academically relevant data with relatively simple administrative procedures (Burns 2002). The ability to discriminate between information that accounts for the distribution of resources and information that details instructional practices (Achilles, Finn, and Pate-Bain 2002) is a foundational skill for school leaders.

Understanding the necessity for data-driven decision making and direct interpretation does not answer the question, "What do we measure?" Student learning and teaching methods are usually at the top of this list; thus, anything that impacts these areas is measured. Moving beyond the standardized tools used to measure schools requires clear learning goals and expectations of schools. Understanding the needs and desires of students, teachers, and other stakeholders requires school leaders to know the expectations, conditions, and circumstances under which the best teaching to optimize the greatest learning occur (Raywid 2002). See Table 2.1.

Evaluation and assessment strategies. Growing emphasis on equality of education for all students requires school leaders to rethink methods of evaluation and assessment. Global methods or the shotgun approach, while not completely

Table 2.1

Specific Goals and Objectives	Specific Expectations of Schools
◆ Learning basic skills (3 Rs) ◆ Learning factual information ◆ Using information ◆ Acquiring desirable habits of mind ◆ Developing character and other desirable traits ◆ Developing individualized talents	◆ Successful schools ◆ Welcoming and user friendly ◆ Fully engaged teachers ◆ Cultivating an environment receptive to student learning ◆ Positive and desirable message

Source: Modified from Raywid 2002.

defunct, are not satisfactory. Democratic principles, emphasizing the achievement of all students, are now demanded as a way of making educators accountable for student achievement, particularly with populations viewed as underserved or underachieving. "No longer can such students be simply prepared for succeeding grades; the emphasis instead must shift to providing the academic skills necessary for success in the remainder of each student's school career, including study skills, assignment completion skills, vocational skills, and the work ethic that will lead students to active participation in contemporary American adult life" (Hargrove et al. 2001).

Determinations about what to measure depend on the context in your school. Using tools that measure student growth, school leaders can develop a repertoire of strategies to accurately determine student achievement of goals that can be graphically articulated (Burns 2002).

Diversity. Diversity in the nation's schools is both an opportunity and a challenge (Banks 2006) requiring school leaders to understand and respond to issues of ethnicity, language, culture, and the special needs of all students. As the number of language-minority students continues to escalate in virtually every school in the United States, an unprecedented effort must be made to prepare teachers and administrators to be adequately prepared to meet this challenge. Given these dramatic statistics, as well as the increases estimated to continue for several decades into the future, it is important to ask how English-language learners are faring in the education system. School leaders seeking to develop a truly diverse organization must be aware of the influence of community. Understanding community requires that leaders appreciate the diversity of culture and to find ways to build connections to each community. School leaders who transform learning environments are proactive in their efforts to create organizations where cultural differences enhance rather than interfere with teaching and learning.

School leaders must work to understand the many complex issues related to diversity and creating environments where every child has the opportunity to be successful, but students must learn methods to learn together; to address and resolve conflicts; to live with others from different cultural, ethnic, and religious backgrounds; and to reconstruct our society to better approximate the democratic ideals found in the Declaration of Independence and our Constitution" (Edgar, Day-Vines, and Patton 2002).

Adult learning principles. Understanding how adults learn is important if school leaders are ultimately responsible for helping to create environments where teachers continue to acquire the skills and knowledge necessary to be effective teachers. Frameworks and methods found in detail in the scholarly, yet practical, teaching models developed by Joyce, Showers, and Calhoun (2006) initially for children and youth can be modified to teach ideas and model to other adults. These include but are not limited to the major components of adult learning—acquisition of knowledge, modeling, practice, observation, and coaching—and can give structure and purpose to teacher development activities. Awareness of the many options available is important in eliminating burnout and indifference to the need for lifelong learning. Capturing the participation of every teacher and administrator is needed to reach a vision of high academic achievement. How does a school leader choose from the many options available? For example, in examining content for online learning, one may ask questions such as: What professional development does the online course offer? What are the technical requirements? Does the curriculum relate to required experiences? Does the curriculum guide students to educationally productive Internet sources? Use questions such as these to facilitate discussions on what the adults in the organization want and need to learn.

Sparks (2002) notes that "large-group 'batch processing' of teachers who are 'talked at' in the name of 'exposing' them to new ideas are ineffective and squander teachers' good will regarding professional development." Engaging adult learners in meaningful activities fulfills their need for authentic learning. School leaders are well advised to heed this principle when planning professional development activities.

Professional development models. The movement to make professional development the responsibility of everyone involved and not a single person or department requires that school leaders be aware of the different approaches available. Understanding these choices and the varying context can assist you in advising teachers or implementing an effective professional development approach.

One approach is to embed professional development in the everyday functions of the school. The authentic task approach (Phlegar and Hurley 1999) and learner-centered professional development are methods that help schools focus on the context and vision in which professional development takes place. The authentic task approach focuses on making learning meaningful for all involved while continuing to expand teaching and learning capacity. Professional development in these frameworks revolves around increasing the ability of schools to improve teaching and learning.

School leaders implementing effective professional development understand that the "goal of all the professionals in a school is to make sure professional development supports both their own and their students' continuous learning opportunities. . . . School improvement happens when a school develops a professional learning community that focuses on student work and changes teaching. . . . In order to do that, you need certain kinds of skills, capacities, and relationships. Those are what professional development can contribute to. . . . Any school that is trying to improve has to think of professional development as a cornerstone strategy" (Fullan 1999). Listed below are some key points to consider when planning professional development (NPEAT 1999):

- ◆ Focus on what students are to learn and how to address the different problems students may have in learning the material.
- ◆ Analyze the difference between (a) actual student performance and (b) goals and standards for student learning.
- ◆ Involve teachers in identifying what they need to learn and in developing the learning experiences in which they will be involved.
- ◆ Make professional development primarily school based and built into the day-to-day work of teaching.
- ◆ Organize professional development around collaborative problem solving.
- ◆ Make professional development continuous and ongoing, with follow-up and support for further learning. Include support from sources external to the school that can provide necessary resources and new perspectives.
- ◆ Incorporate evaluation of multiple sources of information on outcomes for students and on the instruction and other processes involved in implementing lessons learned.
- ◆ Provide opportunities to understand the theory underlying the knowledge and skills being learned.
- ◆ Connect to a comprehensive change process focused on improving student learning.

School leaders need to seek out resources that enable them to not only hear the needs of their staff members but to give ongoing support and feedback about the professional development of every member of the staff. Many organizations such as the National Staff Development Council, have developed standards that should be followed when conducting staff development activities.

Change process. Change is not a project. Tompkins (1995, p. 8) outlines a framework of change process with six phases: skepticism, excitement, acceptance, questioning, disillusion, and dismissal. School leaders who move beyond project change and into systemic change must adopt an articulate, universal, and balanced approach. Ellsworth connects the change process directly to the school leader by creating a framework for change as follows: *Change agents* wish to communicate change, and *change processes* are the methods of instituting the change. School leaders who understand this can begin the process of lasting change but must also be aware of elements that can derail initiatives (Ellsworth 2000).

School leaders who can address the needs of faculties faced with change make it possible for them to "face the severe stresses of adaptive work and the pain of loss that accompanies all fundamental growth and change in human endeavors" (Miller 1996). Moving teachers and students from skepticism to full-fledged adopters requires that you deal with entrenched resistance and "this too will pass" attitudes toward change. Bowman (2000) offers guidance in this area by outlining systemic change as a process evolving through eight consistent stages in sequence if change is to take effect. You will need to understand change, potential inhibitors or disruptors, and how ongoing change is maintained. Solomon (2000), commenting on the "legacy" of changes implemented in an underperforming North Philadelphia school district, said, "Early on, we thought we could simply present stakeholders with data on our students and with explanations about how change can improve students' performance. But we learned that we have to do more. We have to build what I call an appetite for change."

Technology. School leaders in tune with the times understand the importance of not just computers, but digital technology and its potential impact on teaching and learning. Nationally representative data from the National Center for Education Statistics (2001) suggest that in spring 1999, 66 percent of public school teachers were using computers or the Internet for instruction during class time. Addressing those who question why technology, specifically the computer, has had so little impact on measures of academic achievement, Bennett (2000) debunks the myth that teachers have not been trained in how to use technology in their classrooms. He points out that in 2000, the U.S. Department of Education issued a study in which half of all teachers reported that college and graduate work had prepared them to use technology.

It takes time and commitment to address issues of funding, vision support, and the myriad legal issues surrounding the Internet, copyright, file sharing, and child safety. School leaders with the ability to discuss technology and its integration with teachers, students, and other stakeholders can take advantage of the group knowledge available. "Administrators must be prepared for a significant investment of time to move technology from a part-time tool to an active tool fully integrated into the curriculum" (Slowinski 2000).

Management functions. A widening societal gap, an unraveling social fabric, and an increasingly diverse student body have dramatically changed the principal's role. The former bureaucratic model of schooling is insufficient to meet the challenges of a new era (Murphy, Yff, and Shipman 2000). Both the ISLLC and ELCC Standard 2 deal with the principal's task to create a productive learning environment and clearly reflect a drift toward constructivism. "The emphasis has shifted from the nature of learners as passive receivers of information to one in which learners are actively involved in making sense of their own learning" (Ubben, Hughes, and Norris 2001).

Murphy, Yff, and Shipman (2000) state that "competent management, however, is likely to prove insufficient to meet the challenges of leading schools into a new age." The researchers argue that existing structures contribute to many current educational problems and that one way to rectify existing educational problems is to implement the ISLLC Standards, which focus on creating change and developing a professional workplace (Murphy, Yff, and Shipman).

The core purpose of the ISLLC Standards is, according to Richard Elmore "to reconstruct conceptions of authority, status, and school structure to make [educational leaders] instrumental to our most powerful conceptions of teaching and learning" (Murphy, Yff, and Shipman 2000) and thereby develop more responsive schools. The challenge for the school leader, then, is to maintain a proactive stance in terms of molding a positive learning environment. Often, a beginning administrator, burdened with unfamiliar managerial duties, is unlikely to capitalize on his or her most important task: being an instructional leader. At the end of this chapter, we offer a plan intended to improve school culture that you could implement at the beginning of your first year as a school leader.

School cultures. Understanding school cultures requires that school leaders become familiar with processes designed to reveal ". . . working patterns in ways that will be of direct relevance to the improvement of practice in the field" (Angelides and Ainscow 2000).

"One cannot, of course, change a school culture alone. But one can provide forms of leadership that invite others to join as observers of the old and architects of the new" (Barth 2002, p. 1). Involving others in meaningful cultural regeneration requires that school leaders develop skills as prerequisites for success such as group facilitation, individual and group assessments, collaborative methodologies, and self-reflection processes (Norris et al. 2002). School leaders fostering a culture of openness, where normally nondiscussable issues are presented in productive frameworks, are positively impacting academic achievement, staff relations, and community involvement. Be prepared for the unexpected—the introduction of changes to the school's culture will reveal underlying problems.

School leaders must have a level of commitment that carries them beyond thoughts of today. Identification of changes needed in especially "toxic" school cultures push school leaders to change everything now. "In most cases of disenfranchisement, individuals have lost their sense of identity with the organization. They feel cut off from the real purpose and business of the enterprise and react in silence as others carry on the business of education" (Norris et al. 2002). Learning to develop inclusive, active, fully engaged cultures will allow everyone to feel a sense of responsibility for the success of the school.

Essential Elements for School Leaders (ELCC)

Essentials of leadership for ELCC Standard 2 include promoting a positive school culture, providing an effective instructional program, applying best practice to student learning, and designing comprehensive professional growth plans.

Promoting a Positive School Culture

According to Murphy, Yff, and Shipman (2000), the principal's new role is characterized as being "empowering rather than controlling" and as "establishing meaning, rather then directing." It is grounded more on teaching than on informing, more on learning than on knowing, and more on modeling and clarifying values and beliefs than on telling or giving commands. The standards are in harmony with scientific theories that support the idea that sustainable improvements within social systems will occur only when sought and found by the stakeholders themselves (Henderson and Hawthorne 2000). The same idea is advocated by Senge et al. (2000), who suggest that we stop using the bureaucratic, machine-like model for schools and start viewing them as what they are: living systems. The fundamental distinction is that "living systems are self-made while machines are made by others" (p. 53). Similarly, Ubben, Hughes, and Norris (2001) use the brain metaphor to describe a school's contextual framework. The brain metaphor adds an "important dimension of thinking/learning organization. In this context, great emphasis is on shared knowledge and understandings, collaboration, and inquiry."

Effective Learning Cultures

Out of a number of studies, researchers identified four essential aspects characteristic of effective learning cultures: high expectations, safety and order, responsibility and empathy, and praise (Ubben, Hughes, and Norris 2001; Senge et al. 2000).

◆ **High expectations** of students will be met only where learning is purposeful. When learning becomes isolated, alienated, and disconnected from the context of real life, students bury their innate

---

interest in learning and look for answers outside the school's realm, in ways that may not be appropriate or safe.

When educators' capabilities are judged predominantly by their students' scores on standardized tests, a teacher's focus might shift from a nurturing learning environment to more rigorous ways of teaching. However, educators who set standards with the learner's unique talents in mind will see their classes succeeding, without teaching to the test, but simply as a side effect of good teaching.

◆ **Safety and order** are associated with optimal classroom management, in other words, the ability to deal with elements disrupting the learning process. A school that recognizes the dignity of learners gives them appropriate responsibilities. If a child struggles to live up to them, a teacher must not question the delinquent's dignity; instead, the teacher responds with direct respect to the out-of-line behavior, while involving the student in the process of problem solution. Discipline starts and ends with problem solving, not with assumptions about the child. Moreover, disruptive behavior is substantially lessened when the school culture allows for personal contacts between students and their educators. This process of humanization creates a closeness that is required to diminish any feelings of alienation (Ubben, Hughes, and Norris 2001) Avoiding the latter and nurturing a feeling of ownership and belonging contributes considerably to a student's socially responsible conduct.

◆ **Responsibility** for oneself and **empathy** for others depend on learning that is organized around the adolescents' efforts to create their lives. Schools should offer students numerous opportunities to practice making responsible choices about their own learning. A learner who continually jeopardizes the process of education through inappropriate choices needs to be taught how to make responsible decisions. Responsible decision making, in turn, is closely linked with the ability to connect to the environment, in other words, to be empathetic. Empathy helps learners anticipate the consequences of their actions in relation to their own and others' lives. Appropriate teaching methods enhance a student's skills to empathize with his surrounding (Senge et al. 2000).

◆ **Praise** and the mutual expression of appreciation and respect help all stakeholders to recognize their own achievement to the point where it turns into sustaining self-approval (Ubben, Hughes, and Norris 2001).

Applying Best Practice to Student Learning

Teaching and learning are a school's core business. But what does a culture for student learning look like? Who knows the secret ingredients of those successful schools? According to Ubben, Hughes, and Norris (2001), there is no secret to creating a maximally productive culture for student learning. After looking at myriad reports, they identified four essential ingredients:

1. Clear, firm, and high teacher and administrator expectations
2. Consistent rules and consequences that directly relate to breaking the rules
3. A decided and well-implemented emphasis on the self-esteem of all students
4. Public and private acknowledgment and rewarding of positive behavior by students

The third of these four aspects capitalizes on self-esteem. Some researchers (Kohn 1998; Senge et al. 2000), however, challenge the importance of self-esteem in terms of personal success in life, reasoning that "the question of self-esteem is independent from your ability to create what most matters to you in your life" (Senge et al. 2000). Instead, Kohn pinpoints the significance of developing responsibility for and commitment to one's own and others' lives. How can we explain this apparent incongruence?

Persons committed to a task and displaying passion and empathy will support outcomes they care about. Concomitant success guarantees satisfaction and is likely to result in enhanced self-esteem, but not necessarily. It is well known that some of the most successful people in history demonstrated doubt about their skills and talents but were able to achieve their goals.

Self-esteem may be an indicator of an individual's position toward the element in question but must not be viewed as the cause. Responsibility and empathy should be where educators focus (Senge et al. 2000).

A school culture is conducive to student learning only when coupled with certain attitudes and beliefs. Those beliefs are the ones of a transformative educator who perceives schools as living systems with a deeply ingrained ability, need, and desire to learn, thereby bringing forth their own meaningful reality. A transformative leader's philosophy is thus clearly reflected in the way he or she specifies the four "essentials" of positive learning cultures.

Providing an Effective Instructional Program

To develop high expectations for all students requires that educators believe in their students' inherent abilities and innate dignity. The traditional grading system does not allow for a dignified environment when viewing assessment. Students are divided into good and bad or A and F, further suggesting that high expectations cannot be held for those students labeled as below average.

However, if we stop pigeonholing or labeling students as gifted, average, below standard, or disabled, we may be able to see them as just students. Simply, treating students with dignity because it already exists is much like being the great wizard in *The Wizard of Oz* as teacher. Acknowledge, recognize, or highlight and move upward (Senge et al. 2000).

As leaders in the process of learning, we need to build a practice of seeing students for who they are, focusing and integrating the research on multiple intelligences into the lesson plan. In alignment with the federal law, No Child Left Behind, principals must lead teachers to co-create a school where expectations are high for all students. We all know of the Hawthorne effect and high expectations.

Accommodating different learning styles ensures that a student can function in a degree of comfort. This learning approach looks at the child as a whole, building on a student's potential rather than focusing on weaknesses. A nurturing learning environment is supportive and respects the dignity of the learner. A student learns to distinguish between self and the object of what is to be learned; thus, the performance is not associated with a student's self-worth. Students need to be exposed to these real-life experiences "in order to toughen up, build important life muscles," and acquire "the discipline for going the extra mile." Only students with a strong sense of dignity can grow into an adulthood that allows for risk taking and coping with failures.

On the other hand, we will meet our students' high expectations only if learning is purposeful. Senge further elaborates, "For any educator the challenge is to identify the personal vision that motivates and guides the learners and to help create connections between that vision and the learning that needs to occur" (Senge et al. 2000) When learning becomes isolated, alienated, and disconnected from the context of real life, as is often the case in schools capitalizing on drill and rote memorization, it becomes what O'Connor and Bangham (2000) tagged "theater of the absurd."

Holding high expectations must not mean that a school's only focus should be high scores on statewide tests. Schools must both maintain high standards and nurture learning and the learner. Teachers who set high standards and expectations will see real academic success. In professional development, we try to sell the concept that good teaching equals higher achievement, and with higher achievement comes better test scores. This may be problematic as you work more with teachers in a daily school environment where time and temper are often at a minimum.

Since ISLLC Standard 2 is focused on school culture, the safety and order issue will be discussed in the light of classroom management optimal for student progress. Here, the approach to discipline becomes the highest level of concern.

Disruptive behavior is substantially lessened when the school culture allows for personal contacts between students and teachers. Sizer clearly stated that "personalization is the single most important factor that keeps kids in school" (Sizer and Sizer 1999) and Ubben, Hughes, and Norris (2001) suggest that small groups of students should be teamed with particular school officials who serve as advisor(s), becoming responsible for instructional decisions and personalizing learning. This process of humanization creates "the intimacy required to diminish alienation." Avoiding the latter and nurturing a feeling of ownership and belonging contributes considerably to a student's socially responsible conduct. As educators, we soon learn that allowing students to become responsible and held accountable for their actions is respected by both teachers and students when administered fairly. Students have a great sense for fairness and respect when respected (Queen and Algozzine 2007a). Learners who continually jeopardize the process of education through inappropriate choices, such as being absent or engaging in disruptive behavior, must experience consequences in order to learn and make appropriate and responsible decisions.

Responsible decision making, in turn, correlates with the ability of connecting to the environment, in other words, with being empathetic. Empathy helps the learner to anticipate the consequences of his actions in relation to his and to others' lives. Appropriate teaching methods can enhance a student's skills to empathize with his surroundings.

The skills students need in a contemporary setting are in most cases competencies associated with computers and rapidly changing technology. The schools must not hesitate to teach these increasingly imperative skills.

Positive learning cultures are characterized "by outward and readily recognized mutual expressions of appreciation and respect ... honestly given and graciously received" (Ubben, Hughes, and Norris 2001). The same authors stress that the efficacy of public acknowledgment of achievement must not be underestimated. "The point is that praise, sincerely given, works." It is critical to help all stakeholders recognize their own achievement to the point where it turns into sustaining self-approval.

Designing Comprehensive Professional Growth Plans

Faced with a stack of papers viewed as unfamiliar managerial work, a beginning principal is unlikely to take a proactive stance as an instructional leader, unless a specific plan for staff development is in place. The plan we suggest at the end of this chapter (Tables 2.3 through 2.5) accommodates three essential areas: fostering a collegial atmosphere that allows for productive teamwork and a risk-taking attitude, accommodating the children's dignity and diversity, and generating an environment that minimizes interference with the process of learning.

The succession—collegiality followed by dignity followed by discipline—is intentional. The creation of a risk-free environment and collegial atmosphere becomes a prerogative for any further developments. In the first year of staff training, teachers need to be assured that potential failures and setbacks are normal alongside the process of school renewal. A collegial climate fosters mutual trust and courage among the school's constituents. In addition, critical thinking and skeptical attitudes, which only evolve in a climate of trust, are expected and appreciated as valuable contributors to the institution's reconstruction. Once cohesiveness is taking roots, the next step can be implemented.

During the second year, the emphasis is placed on changing perspective and gradually making adults see the dignity of the children entrusted to the school. The recognition of the learner's dignity, in turn, is prerequisite for a teacher's meaningful engagement with children who struggle with psychological issues. Also, the plan must display the school leader's knowledge about the initiation of change. Lasting alterations will take place only if the actors want this to occur, and not because they need to be implemented. Thus, the individual's awareness of the problem becomes prevalent and likely to promote greater willingness. Then the knowledge of how to induce desired alterations will quicken a person's commitment to change. In summation, awareness/willingness, knowledge/readiness, and commitment follow a logical progression in the process of effective change implementation (Ubben, Hughes, and Norris 2001).

Most important, the staff development plan (Tables 2.3 through 2.5) accounts for the following specifics of ISLLC Standard 2 (ISLLC 1996):

- Professional development is an integral part of school improvement.
- Professional development promotes a focus on student learning consistent with the school vision and goals.
- Student and staff feel valued and important.
- A variety of sources of information is used to make decisions.
- The school culture and climate are assessed on a regular basis.
- Multiple sources of information regarding performance are used by staff and students.
- A variety of supervisory and evaluation models is employed.

As principal, you can expect to have sufficient latitude at your site to initiate change. The success of change, however, is buttressed by three pillars: guiding ideas, organizational arrangements, and methods and tools. Mutually shared guiding ideas are essential to sustaining change. Cognizant of the importance of organizational arrangements, you must provide the necessary resources: appropriate decision-making structures, policies, allocation of space and time, feedback and communication mechanisms, and planning processes. The tools and methods you offer as the instructional leader will trigger the faculty's and staff's readiness and capabilities to buy into and prompt the process of school renewal.

Finally, the question arises how Standard 2 is linked into the above-stated four aspects of successful learning communities. Table 2.2 compares the four essential aspects with the specifics of ISLLC Standard 2.

Table 2.2

How the Four Essentials of Successful Schools Relate to ISLLC Standard 2

Essential Aspects	ISLLC Standard 2
1. Expectations High expectations can only be the result of concomitant underlying assumptions. These assumptions reflect, first, the *dignity* of a child and, second, the belief that *every child can learn*. Only a teacher whose educational philosophy is grounded in these two fundamental beliefs will establish high expectations for all children. Moreover, expectations can be met only if we apply teaching methods that have proven to be conducive to student learning.	◆ Student growth and development ◆ Applied learning theories ◆ Diversity and its meaning for educational programs ◆ The role of technology in promoting student learning and professional growth ◆ The proposition that all students can learn ◆ The variety of ways in which students can learn ◆ The benefits that diversity brings to the school community ◆ Diversity is considered in developing learning experiences, and there is a culture for high expectations for self, student, and staff performance ◆ Multiple opportunities to learn are available to all students ◆ The school is organized for success
2. Safety and Order Ubben, Hughes, and Norris (2001, p. 98) state that they had never visited a productively operating school that did not have a safe and orderly environment. This aligns with Maslow's hierarchy of needs (Lunenburg and Ornstein 2000), which asserts that needs and concomitant motivations emerge only if more basic needs are satisfied. Since	◆ Principles of effective instruction ◆ School cultures ◆ A safe and supportive learning environment ◆ Barriers to student learning are identified, clarified, and addressed *(continued)*

Essential Aspects	ISLLC Standard 2
2. Safety and Order *(concluded)* safety and order accommodate the needs most important to the individual, they must be tended to before productive learning can occur. Thus, reasonable classroom rules and their consistent and fair enforcement ensure an environment that allows for effective student learning.	
3. Responsibility and Empathy Teachers who see the dignity in their students communicate high expectations, respect, empathy, and an unconditional positive regard for them. If necessary, they apply appropriate negative consequences, because they care about students who demonstrate "out-of-line" behavior. These educators are committed to transforming students into responsible citizens who care about themselves and others and demonstrate the ability of and motivation for life long learning. Action-oriented programs convey contents that are relevant and engaging for the learner and account for the need of self-actualization.	◆ Lifelong learning for self and others ◆ Preparing students to be contributing members of society ◆ Individuals arc treated with fairness, dignity, and respect ◆ Student and staff feel valued and important ◆ Lifelong learning is encouraged and modeled ◆ Technologies are used in teaching and learning ◆ Student learning is assessed using a variety of techniques
4. Praise According to Ubben, Hughes, and Norris (2001), "positive learning environments are characterized by outward and readily recognized mutual expressions of appreciation and respect . . . honestly given and graciously received." These authors	◆ Measurement, evaluation, and assessment strategies ◆ The contributions and responsibilities of each individual are acknowledged *(continued)*

Essential Aspects	ISLLC Standard 2
4. Praise (*concluded*) write that praise works. At some point in life, the vast majority of people depend on extrinsic rewards for their personal accomplishments. Appreciation in these moments reaffirms and may actually help to reinforce the feeling of success that is crucial to sustaining the motivation for further developments.	◆ Student and staff accomplishments are recognized and celebrated

Suggested Readings

Hessel, K., and J. Holloway. 2001. *A Framework for School Leaders: Linking the ISLLC Standards to Practice.* Princeton, NJ: Educational Testing Service.

Joyce, Showers, and Calhoun 2006 *Models of Teaching.* Boston: Pearson Education.

Tanner, D., and L. Tanner, 2007 *Curriculum Theory and Practice.* Upper Saddle River, NJ: Prentice Hall.

Suggested Activities

1. Put into a narrative form what the staff development plan that follows is striving to achieve. What are the strengths of the plan? The weaknesses? What changes would you make as a principal? Would it be different at the elementary, middle, and high school levels? Why or why not?

Table 2.3

Staff Developement Model Plan

Year 1: Collaboration
Goal: To build groups where professionals collaborate in a collegial manner.

	Objectives/ Question	Procedures	Schedule	Instruments/ Materials Used
Awareness	How collegial is the staff?	Survey among teachers and all other staff	September	

Staff Developement Model Plan *(continued)*

	Objectives/ Question	Procedures	Schedule	Instruments/ Materials Used
Awareness	Why is collegiality important?	Present survey data Exchange personal experiences	October	Thought-provoking materials
	How should change occur? Get to know your colleagues	Two-day workshop	October	Personal mastery Team learning
Readiness	What is the difference between congeniality and collegiality?	In-service Invite teachers with team experiences Visit team-managed schools	November/ December	
	Who collaborates with whom?	Build groups	December	
Commitment	How can we benefit from each other?	Peer observation Interdisciplinary teaching Team teaching	January/ February	
	What did we learn?	Groups present and share their experiences with faculty	March	
Assessment	Did collegiality improve?	Survey Data from presentation	April	
	How can we further improve collegiality? Do groups need to be rearranged?	Survey Research Expert advice Data from presentation	April	

Table 2.4

Staff Developement Model Plan *(continued)*

Year 2: Dignity/Learning Styles

Goal: "Professionals work together to explore basic knowledge about learning, memory, attention, and motivation in a practical manner, instead of focusing on technique without a sound theoretical basis" (Senge 2000).

	Objectives/ Question	Procedures	Schedule	Instruments/ Materials Used
Awareness	How do I see a learning classroom?	Teachers outline their ideas individually and discuss them in their teams	September	Designing a learning classroom
Awareness	What would it bring me?	Teacher discussion in teams Hand in short essay	September	
Readiness	The dignity of the child	Individual reading Open circle training	October	Open circle
Readiness	Introducing eight intelligences	In-service Invite teachers to do 4MAT training	October	4MAT system
Readiness	Screening your students with 4MAT	Evaluate and hand in screening results	October	4MAT software
Commitment	Expand teachers' repertoire of instructional techniques	Two-day workshop Teachers introduce each other to various techniques	November	Models of Teaching (Joyce, Weil, and Calhoun 2006)
Commitment	Designing a learning classroom Individual reading	Hand in personal suggestion for improvements in classroom	December	Designing a learning classroom (Senge 2000)
Commitment	How successful are my suggestions?	Implementing suggestion in the classroom	January/ February	

Staff Developement Model Plan *(continued)*

	Objectives/ Question	Procedures	Schedule	Instruments/ Materials Used
Assessment	What works for me/for us?	Evaluate personal experiences and share with team and faculty	March	
	How can we further support learning classrooms?	Evaluate: Survey among faculty TPAI data and make suggestions/seek expert advice	April	

Table 2.5

Staff Developement Model Plan *(continued)*

Year 3: Discipline

Goal: "Building a learning community for children means giving them responsibilities and realizing that children who are struggling with some of the psychological issues, for lack of a better term, are not going to do their work just because they are supposed to do their work" (Senge 2000).

	Objectives/ Question	Procedures	Schedule	Instruments/ Materials Used
Awareness	Why is good classroom management important?	Survey Principal presents data on discipline problems (referrals, suspensions, dropouts)	September	
	Who has what kind of discipline problems?	Identify three major problems Share experiences in groups Group presentations	September	

Staff Developement Model Plan *(continued)*

	Objectives/ Question	Procedures	Schedule	Instruments/ Materials Used
Awareness	What needs to stop? What needs to be improved? What should be continued regarding classroom management?	Outline personal goals regarding discipline problems	September	
Readiness	What works? Introducing RCM	Visit RCM school In-service with RCM	October	Thought-provoking material RCM handbook
	How do we implement it at the school?	Principal communicates RCM policies and rules that will start in January	November	
	How do I implement Reclaiming Classroom Management in my classroom? (RCM) (Queen and Algozzine 2007a)	Outline reactions to your three major discipline problems State rules/laws	November	
Commitment	Get used to RCM	Teachers implement RCM in their classrooms	December	
	RCM becomes a schoolwide policy	Principal and teachers implement RCM at the school	Beginning January 1...	

Staff Developement Model Plan *(continued)*

	Objectives/ Question	Procedures	Schedule	Instruments/ Materials Used
Assessment	How successful was imple- mentation?	Teacher Survey Disciplinary data Teams make suggestions for improvements	April	
	What needs to be improved?	Suggestions for next year Talk to RCM specialist	April	

MAJOR CHAPTER ASSIGNMENT:
Curriculum Design and Standard 2

Pretend the class is a group of principals who are working together as the leadership team for a new charter school that has been outlined in three levels of curriculum and instruction. The state has given a waiver to the school, and no specific course of study has to be followed. Listed below is the only document your faculty will receive. Develop a plan of how leadership team can implement the model (which includes just examples) at Levels II and III. Be creative and operate within the focus and intention of ISLLC and ELCC II .

Vision Statement

It is our vision to grow together to where our school structure becomes the model for the schools of the decade 2010.

Mission Statement

Our mission is to guide students along the career paths that best suit their aspira- tions and evolving individual skills. We hope to fulfill this through a multidi- mensional, multicultural, and pluralistic program and environment that will be adaptable to an ever-changing society.

Curriculum Design Standard 2 *(continued)*

Level I Goals

Goal 1: Adaptability

Upon completion of Grade 12 at Queen City Secondary School, the student has demonstrated the ability to adapt to a constantly changing environment in an ever-evolving world.

Goal 2: Higher-Order Problem Solving

Upon completion of Grade 12 at Queen City Secondary School, the student has demonstrated:

1. The ability to identify the source of a problem in his or her environment and/or within himself or herself.
2. The ability to create realistic, adaptable solutions to problems facing him or her in a vastly changing world using sound judgment.
3. The successful execution of a problem that shows applicable and quantitative results in which the effectiveness of the solution can be measured.

Goal 3: Acceptance/Diversity

Upon completion of Grade 12 at Queen City Secondary School, the student has demonstrated acceptance of and gained the desire to understand the diversity of various cultural backgrounds.

Level II Goals

Program Goals

Upon completion of each program area, the student has demonstrated the following:

IA. *Adaptability (Content).* The ability to select and learn appropriate content.

IIA. *Higher-Order Problem Solving (Content).* The ability to integrate the content and processes of each program area into a higher level of understanding.

IIIA. *Acceptance/Diversity (Content).* The ability to contrast and compare without bias the values and traditions of other cultures to his or her own.

IB. *Adaptability (Social).* The ability to adapt to and accept other points of view in an ever-changing society.

IIB. *Higher-Order Problem Solving (Social).* The ability to recognize and analyze social issues in order to create equitable solutions.

IIIB. *Acceptance/Diversity (Social).* The ability to respond to various opinions through the development of diplomatic skills.

Curriculum Design Standard 2 *(continued)*

IC. *Adaptability (Individual).* The ability to adapt to various situations.

IIC. *Higher-Order Problem Solving (Individual).* The ability to analyze and discover one's true identity.

IIIC. *Acceptance/Diversity (Individual).* The ability to accept the many cultures of a diverse society while continuing to focus on one's own individuality.

Instructional Goals

In accordance with the program goals, students will

IA. *Adaptability (Content)*

1. Develop skills in evaluating and analyzing content.

2. Develop mastery of a variety of learning strategies and/or styles such as

   a. discussion

   b. computer

   c. inquiry

   d. textbooks

3. Develop diplomatic/debating skills.

4. Work cooperatively in a group using skills such as

   a. listening

   b. playing

   c. following procedures

   d. using diplomatic behavior

   e. debating

IIA. *Higher-Order Problem Solving (Content)*

1. Develop the ability to decide which content skills and processes are best suited to particular problem-solving contexts. Some abilities needed to perform:

   a. ability to draw from previously learned skills and knowledge

   b. ability to perform previously learned skills and knowledge

   c. knowledge of several different content areas

2. Become adept at using skills from other content areas in new and different situations. To be able to do this, students should already:

   a. understand how skills are interchangeable

   b. have practiced overlapping content areas

3. Develop the ability to understand, learn, accept, and then integrate new information as part of a whole knowledge system.

Curriculum Design Standard 2 *(continued)*

IIIA. *Acceptance/Diversity (Content)*

1. Be able to identify personal and/or learned stereotypes and their sources. Skills needed include

   a. ability to distinguish between fact and fiction

   b. ability to replace old stereotypes with new, accurate information

2. Develop investigational skills needed to reveal all angles of a situation. Included are the following:

   a. library/media research

   b. interviewing

   c. community involvement

3. Develop sound judgmental skills. Needed to perform sound

   a. judgment:

   b. ability to see different points of view

   c. ability to distinguish between fact and fiction

   d. empathy

   e. a sense of fairness

IB. *Adaptability (Social)*

1. Develop skills to adapt to various points of view.

2. Develop acceptance skills to get along with and form relation ships with those different from themselves. These skills include

   a. listening

   b. questioning

   c. understanding

   d. planning

11B. *Higher-Order Problem Solving (Social)*

Develop analytical skills to create quantitative and qualitative solutions through the following skills: Mathematical

   a. problem-solving techniques

   b. procedures

   c. inquiry

   d. discussion

Curriculum Design Standard 2 *(continued)*

IIIB. Acceptance/Diversity (Social)

Develop skills that adjust and respond to different points of view through

    a. listening

    b. discussion

    c. cooperation

    d. questions

IC. Adaptability (Individual)

1. Develop skills in adapting to different situations, such as

    a. Being exposed to many common situations

    b. Learning how to handle oneself in different situations

2. Develop a mastery of different disciplines. Students should do as many of the following as possible:

    a. enroll in academic classes

    b. enroll in vocational classes

3. Develop the ability to listen to those who are different from oneself.

IIC. Higher-Order Problem Solving (Individual)

1. Develop skills to analyze different situations and learn how to create proper solutions.

2. Learn about various career choices in order to be able to skillfully choose a good career path for oneself.

IIIC. Acceptance/Diversity (Individual)

1. Learn about the various cultures in our society. Skills needed include

    a. research and exploration skills

    b. ability to replace previously learned stereotypes with new, accurate information

2. Develop skills for discovering oneself, such as

    a. understanding one's true cultural background

    b. understanding how one's cultural history interacted with other diverse groups' histories

3. Develop skills to stand up for one's individuality. These skills include

    a. participation in debates

    b. voicing one's opinion while respecting those of others

3

Standard Three: Management as an Essential of Leadership Development

Although researchers stress the importance of the principal as instructional leader, the consensus in the literature is that principals spend most of their time dealing with managerial issues.

—Michael E. Doyle and Donna M. Rice

ISLLC Standard 3	ELCC Standard 3
A school administrator is an educational leader who promotes the success of all students by ensuring management of the organization, operations, and resources for a safe, efficient, and effective learning environment.	*Candidates who complete the program are educational leaders who have the knowledge and ability to promote the success of all students by managing the organization, operations, and resources in a way that promotes a safe, efficient, and effective learning environment.*

Certainly, as Doyle and Rice (2002) stated, a school principal will spend a great deal of energy on managerial duties. But if a strong framework is in place, the time spent on management will diminish, allowing the principal to focus on the instructional part of the job. The ISLLC and ELCC Standards 3 indicate the necessary management characteristics for school administrators. A principal is accountable for managing a school in a sound, organized manner so the daily routines are not interrupted by problems preventing teachers from maximizing instruction. In essence, the school leader is the human resources manager, the operations manager, and the chief financial officer of the building. Underscoring the importance of this role is the projection that new administrators will replace as many as 25 percent of practicing principals who are eligible for retirement in the next several years (Lauder 2000).

Essential elements of leadership for Standard 3 include management of the organization, management of operations, and management of resources. Leaders should be knowledgeable in the following areas: organizational theory, models of organizations, principles of organizational development, school safety, human resource management, human resource development, fiscal operations, school management, and school facilities. We will address these areas, and then turn to managing the organization, operations, and resources. Finally, we will look at the framework of promoting a safe, efficient, and effective learning environment.

Essential Knowledge for School Leaders

Morgan (1997) views the classical model of management as being more of a process of planning and organization, which has elements of command, coordination, and control included. These components form the framework for the basic techniques managers use in MBO (management by objective), PPBS (planning, programming, budgeting systems), and other structured methods of management.

Piquero and Simpson (2002) present complexity theory as a way of explaining organizations, their complexity, and behavior in context. They also look at rational choice as management's decision-making process to explain the actions of managers and subordinates. Lunenburg and Ornstein (2004) state that classical organizational theories consist of both scientific and administrative management–related components. Scientific management, based on the beliefs of Frederick Taylor's experiences in the steel industry, has evolved into four basic principles: scientific job analysis, selection of personnel, management cooperation, and functional supervising.

Again, in administrative management, the direction in classical organizational theory comes from business management theorists such as Henri Fayol, Luther Gulick, and Max Weber. Administrative management focuses on the management of the entire organization (Lunenberg and Ornstein 2004). Fayol, Gulick, and Weber developed different but similar ideas of how an organization should be effectively operated by identifying important functions of a manager. The seven major administrative functions of a principal became planning, organizing, staffing, directing, coordinating, reporting, and budgeting.

In order to improve the running of factories during the 19th and early 20th centuries, foremen or supervisors were separated from factory floor workers. Likewise, schools were established with the principal as foreman and the teacher as the factory floor worker, even though many early elementary school principals often had a classroom as well as being principal. Communication trickled from the top down, and the principals were ultimately detached from the actual teaching of children. The focus of the early theorists was on the actual task of work, not the worker and the customer, whereas in today's industrial and educational environment the focus is based on outcomes.

Since the focus on education has changed from the early years, educational leaders today must be knowledgeable about the current philosophies in organizational management. Many schools, districts, and states have mandated site-based management (SBM). The theory behind SBM is decentralization of decision–making and placing a shared capacity for the process as close to the school level as possible. Decentralization, in theory, gives schools what McAdams refers to as "agility," the ability to succeed in a rapidly changing world. The four major characteristics of an agile organization are enriching the customer, cooperating to enhance competitiveness, organizing to master change and uncertainty, and leveraging the impact of people and information (McAdams 1997). Under SBM, the principal as the school and school community's representative presents a school improvement plan to the superintendent, and together the two leaders further align the plan with the district's vision. School leaders with an understanding of a decentralized framework can reap the benefits.

School leaders must also beware. In *Images of Organization* (1997), Gareth Morgan outlines the many metaphors currently used to explain organizational theory. He warns, "We have to accept that any theory or perspective that we bring to the study of organization and management, while capable of creating valuable insights, is also incomplete, biased, and potentially misleading."

Models of organizations. Educational leaders have to develop a deep understanding of the school organization. Understanding the operating processes such as SBM, Total Quality Management (TQM), Participatory Management Model (PMM), Systems Thinking, or Six Sigma is only a part of the picture. Answering the question of "What type of organization is this?" is essential for leaders to implement innovations or initiatives.

Most models fit into one of the following basic forms. Henry Mintzberg (1989) outlines five organizational structures: simple structure, machine bureaucracy, professional bureaucracy, divisionalized form, and adhocracy. Gareth Morgan (1997) presents organizational models as metaphors: machine, organic, brain, culture, political, psychic, flux, and transformation. By viewing a school as a social system, Jacob Getzels and Egon Guba developed an idea of a model

Figure 3.1

The Getzels-Guba Model

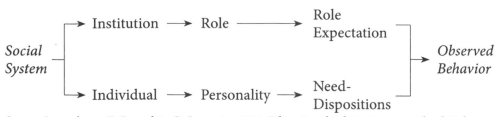

Source: Lunenburg, F. C., and A. C. Ornstein. 2004. *Educational Administration,* 4th ed. Belmont: Wadsworth/Thomson Learning.

involving two independent and interactive parts of the system. The schools have a certain role in the organization, and the individual teachers and administrators have another role. As viewed in Figure 3.1, both groups work independently of each other as well with each other toward one purpose (Lunenburg and Ornstein 2004, p. 73).

Principles of organizational development. Developing productive schools at minimal costs, making the best use of financial and human resources at the same time, and meeting the need for accountability are just some of the considerations as school leaders build and maintain organizations. School leaders need to know the norms within an organization and the reasons why the norms are in place. Developing an understanding of how positive organizational cultures are formed can help reveal the motives behind actions. Leaders can use the information to understand the reasons the decisions affect the behavior of the organization and individuals and groups within it. Limited program evaluations will not provide the information to address fundamental organizational traits and characteristics that influence all programs. Torres and Preskill warned in 1998 and strongly advised against such limited or "one-shot" approaches.

School leaders taking on the challenge of developing an organization that will accomplish its mission must be willing to challenge the existing paradigms present in the organization and develop supports that facilitate necessary changes. Today, these dynamic structures are often developed into "learning organizations," a term often credited to Peter Senge. Marked by their use of innovation, learning organizations move through five stages in their development or implementation of change as labeled by Torres and Preskill in 2001:

◆ Status quo or the traditional.

◆ Awareness of a need to change and exploration of a new approach.

◆ Transitioning to an organizational learning approach.

- Adoption and implementation of an organizational learning approach.
- Predominance and refinement of the approach.

School safety. Managing the school environment and ensuring the safety of students and staff allows the business of instruction and learning to occur. Children will test the limits of established rules, often leading to classroom or school disruptions. By having guidelines and procedures in place for such instances, teachers and principals can usually deal with the matter quickly and efficiently without major disruptions to the learning process.

In the early years of education, corporal punishment was used as a means of dealing with misbehavior. The headmaster or teachers used a switch to punish, not change, the behavior of the malcontent. In the late 20th century, many educators moved away from using corporal punishment as a means of changing behavior because the act only punished the child and didn't change the behavior. Incredibly, in the early years of the 21st century, 23 states still allow corporal punishment in schools (http://library.thinkquest.org/J002606/).

With today's changing society, many children are not taught concepts of behavior that mirror a community's values, and therefore they enter school without an understanding of socially acceptable behavior. In almost every *Phi Delta Kappan* Gallup poll of public attitudes toward public schools for at least the past decade, researchers found the public believes schools should be teaching students to be responsible citizens, that values and discipline should be taught by the schools, and that schools should handle discipline problems. We must point out that discipline and safe schools still rank in the top concerns by parents and teachers.

Educators are constantly reminded of the importance of school safety with events such as those in Jonesboro, Arkansas; Littleton, Colorado; and Red Lake, Minnesota. Albert Snow (2003) suggests the following strategies as ways to deal with school safety:

- Be fair and consistent with every discipline decision that you make.
- Have a schoolwide discipline plan.
- Go to a 4×4 block schedule at the high school.
- Make teachers discipline their students.
- Call parents about discipline problems.
- Document your discipline problems.
- Do not make discipline policies that you are not going to enforce.
- Remove graffiti from the school immediately.
- Have a crisis management plan in place.
- Have your school evaluated for safety.
- Enclose your school as much as possible.

- Consider school uniforms.
- Consider school ID badges for students and teachers.
- Be prepared to deal with a student with a weapon.
- Be prepared to deal with the search of a student.

Queen and Algozzine (2007) reported from their recent decade-long study of a single school system in North Carolina that school problems and classroom disruptions were improved by 38 percent when on a 4×4 block model and the percentage almost doubled when the block was used with a strong, schoolwide discipline plan such as the Responsibility Classroom Management (RCM) Plan.

Although the public's perception that school safety is the number one concern has dropped to second place, according to the 36th annual *Phi Delta Kappan* Gallup poll (2005 and 2006), school leaders must remain vigilant in the pursuit of school safety. And school safety is not only internal. The reader is reminded of two major episodes in the early fall of 2006 where adult males entered the schools and molested and killed girls in a traditional environment in Colorado and in a peace-centered culture in the Amish community in Pennsylvania. Principals must strive to use all legal means to keep the students safe and be alert to possible attacks by nonschool individuals or terrorist groups, while not forgetting the internal nightmares of killing by disgruntled students from within the school.

Human resource management and development. "Employees in high-performance work organizations are expected to be committed to organizational goals, to work in teams, and to perform various tasks; these include traditional managerial tasks, such as team-based planning and decision making" (Streumer 1999, p. 2). School leaders who understand and effectively manage the relationships among climate, performance, and resource management will be able to bring about dramatic improvement in goal attainment while ensuring opportunities for growth in the school and its personnel. School leaders searching for ways to enhance the ability of each individual to contribute to the achievement of goals and missions must create "organizations that support their employees by developing effective policies based on ability, motivation, and opportunity and create higher levels of organizational commitment, motivation, and job satisfaction" (Purcell, Kinnie, and Hutchinson 2003). Albert Snow writes in *Practical Advice for Administrators* that a stressed-out teacher is not providing effective instruction, and therefore the principal must provide opportunities for the teacher's self-confidence to be renewed or reassured. One of your main responsibilities as principal is to make recommendations to hire and fire, not counting the daily duties of managing all certified and noncertified staff in the school. The community's perception of how good or bad a school is comes from interactions with school personnel. Therefore, the way you handle staffing is a key part of successful leadership (Snow 2003). The human resources role is primarily to build relationships between the leader and the teachers, among the teachers, and between the teachers and the students that enable risk taking, coaching, and giving and receiving feedback and reflections to guide improvement. The quality of such relationships in a school is an indicator of the learning environment (Taylor 2002, p. 43).

Fiscal operations. Sound fiscal practices and understanding will have a direct impact on student achievement. Every business has a chief financial officer (CFO)—and the school's is the principal. In the area of school finance, fiscal responsibility demands that you as principal make sure every detail is aboveboard. Mismanagement of funds is the number one reason principals are fired. Monies must be distributed equitably so that all teachers and students benefit. While ensuring that the distribution of funds throughout the organization is justified by need, you must be prepared to steer funds where they will directly improve teaching and learning (Picus 2000). Funds must be examined so all instructional materials are purchased to meet the needs of the defined curriculum. You must look at cost-effective ways to reach the academic goals of the school. According to Gerald Bracey, Krueger's most recent study did find that "society gets back about $2 for every dollar invested in small classes" (Bracey 2001). As the financial leader, you must have the know-how to look for ways to bring outside financial help to the school within the confines of the system's guidelines in order to create a partnership with the community to ultimately reach the academic goals established by the school. Understanding the fiscal operations of schools, districts, and state and federal entities will help school leaders make these decisions (Association for Supervision and Curriculum Development 1995). Unfortunately, few classes in the principal training programs help in this area. While not nearly as complicated as the management of funds that superintendents have to monitor, central offices have personnel to assist with this massive task. We suggest that you interview some principals and discuss in class the items you will have to deal with at the various levels of elementary, middle, and secondary schools as a principal. Most schools have a financial secretary that maintains records and reports, but it is the principal who is held accountable, not only professionally but personally as well. Make sure you have the right help and get sufficient background checks before recommending hiring a financial assistant or secretary.

School facilities. On any given school day, about 20 percent of Americans spend time in a school building. The average age of our school buildings is close to 50 years, and studies by the U.S. General Accounting Office have documented widespread physical deficiencies in many of them (Schneider 2002). As the operations supervisor of the school building, you must pay attention to details, ensuring that the heating/cooling system is in order, the fire alarms as well as the extinguishers work, and the floors and windows are clean. The school's appearance reflects the principal's values and priorities. Even an older schoolhouse can be kept clean, neat, and in good working condition for the students. The principal generally does not personally perform the functions of plumber or janitor, but the bottom line is the principal makes sure all the day-to-day routines and equipment are in good order so children may come to school to learn and teachers come to teach in a safe school environment.

The physical environment can be considered as the second teacher for the students, since space has the power to organize and promote pleasant relationships between people of different ages, to provide changes, to promote choices and activities, and to spark different types of social, cognitive, and affective learning. You can involve faculty, community, and other stakeholders in a constructive analysis of the efficient use of facilities (Sanoff, Pasalar, and Hashas 2001).

Essential Elements for School Leaders (ELCC Standards)

Managing the Organization

Effectively managing the organization of the school is the most important task in the mastery of Standard 3, but within this role the principal's major responsibility and goal is measured by the degree of learning attained by the students, more recently the level of performance on state tests. Part of achieving this goal is the effective retention and professional development of the licensed staff, because without a highly qualified teaching faculty dedicated to improving student success, learning cannot and will not take place. In today's society, the measure of a school's success is based on how well the school performed on the state testing and is published in local newspapers for the public to judge.

In a report written by the Department of Labor, a principal is described in the following manner: "Educational administrators set educational standards and goals and establish the policies and procedures to carry them out. They also supervise managers, support staff, teachers, counselors, librarians, coaches, and others. They develop academic programs, monitor students' educational progress, train and motivate teachers and other staff, manage guidance and other student services, administer recordkeeping, prepare budgets, handle relations with parents, prospective and current students, employers, and the community, and perform many other duties" (stats.bls.gov 2004).

All the outside stressors have made the job more difficult and discouraged teachers from taking positions in administration. Principals are now being held more accountable for the performance of students and teachers, and at the same time for adhering to a growing number of government regulations such as No Child Left Behind (NCLB) (stats.bls.gov). While principals have traditionally been accountable for performing competently, today's accountability of "high standard for all students" usually translates into "high test scores for all students" (Lashway 2000, p. 9). The new level of accountability involves far more than testing, according to the Southern Regional Education Board, which has described accountability as a system of five closely linked processes: high standards set the target, standards and assessments are aligned, assessment results are made public, failure to meet high standards has consequences, and professional development is a priority.

All this leaves the principal in a very tough situation. National, state and district mandates prescribe targeted outcomes demanding the best of instructional leaders. What can the principal do to control the daily managerial duties and focus on instruction?

In a study by the National Association of Secondary School Principals (NASSP) and the National Association of Elementary School Principals (NAESP), Ubben, Hughes and Norris (2001) described six abilities important to the success of management by principals:

- The ability to plan and organize work.
- The ability to work with and lead others.
- The ability to analyze problems and make decisions.
- The ability to communicate orally and in writing.
- The ability to perceive the needs and concerns of others.
- The ability to perform under pressure.

A principal with excellent management qualities will deal with issues firmly and promptly and have a system in place to take care of any problems. Effective school leaders create a school where daily activities occur without their continuous engagement. As principal, your main job is to produce circumstances where the school operations can be changed at a moment's notice to meet the changing demands of a situation (Ubben, Hughes, and Norris 2001).

The organizational structure of an efficient school must include the school's community members. Together, the team develops the school's vision, mission, and goals, instituting high expectations for the students, staff, and school (Brost 2000). The principal's role is to guide individuals to be committed members of a collaborative decision-making unit (Lunenburg and Ornstein 2000). In your role as principal, you must be a skilled decision maker as well as adept at helping groups come to a consensus. In addition, you must be knowledgeable and/or have expertise concerning the problem or issue being presented for a decision. Collective decision making allows for many to feel ownership with the decisions of the organization whereby there is less opportunity for dissension.

Lunenburg and Ornstein (2000) illustrate the authority-driven organizational structure typically found in middle and high schools in Figure 3.2:

The authors must quickly add that many elementary school principals do not have assistant principals and department chairs. This is usually based on

Figure 3.2

School Organizational Chart

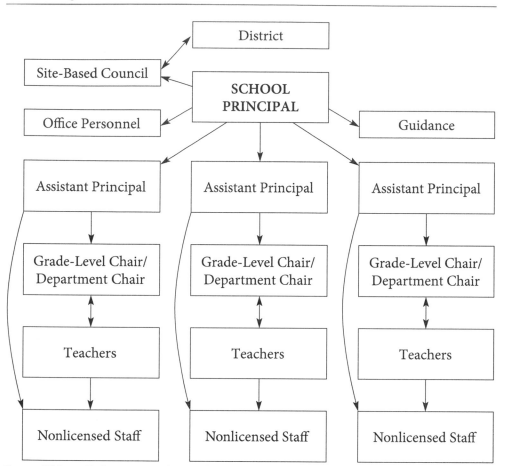

Source: Ubben, G. C., L. W. Hughes, and C. J. Norris. 2001. *The Principal: Creative Leadership for Effective Schools,* 4th ed. Boston: Allyn and Bacon.

either a state or district formula. Even so, the wise principal will delegate some responsibility of leadership to grade-level team leaders.

The hierarchy shown above in Figure 3.2 represents responsibility, and if shared decision making at the school community level is not authentic, the hierarchy will be perceived as the way decisions are made.

Traditionally, the principal delegates responsibilities to assistant principals. The assistant principals are offered a dotted line to the subsequent staff under them on the organizational chart, while the principal has a solid line, representing the final authority. The office staff and guidance staff receive direction from the administration as a whole. Departmental chairs and grade-level team leaders, under the principal's direction, should direct teachers or noncertified staff to take roles of responsibility for particular projects. Noncertified staff include teaching assistants as well as custodians, bus drivers, and cafeteria employees. There are some occasions when a dotted line might appear between those roles and the teachers, but in a fashion similar to that of the chairs and teachers, purely in a managerial manner (Lunenburg and Ornstein 2000).

Designating specific roles to individuals for particular responsibilities is crucial to a school's efficiency. Responsibilities are not lessening—indeed, quite the opposite—so it is imperative for the efficiency of the school for principals to develop decision-making teams and school staffs with clearly defined roles and responsibilities (Miller, A. W. 2001).

Managing Operations

One of a principal's most essential skills is the ability to communicate effectively. According to Ubben, Hughes, and Norris (2001, p. 320), "communication is the glue that binds the learning community together." Principals need the school operations to run efficiently; therefore, problem-solving skills are a must. According to Stephen Covey, no problem can be solved without first having communication and a mutual understanding of the problem. Effective communication is essential for schools to operate efficiently. Effective communication must be practiced and based on mutual trust (Covey 2004).

Hoy and Sweetland (2001) looked at schools as typical bureaucracies. The researchers concluded from their study that bureaucracies that used "interactive dialogue" created enabling, as opposed to coercive, environments. The authentic, open communication builds a foundation of trust, allowing organizations to operate efficiently. Communication is difficult and taxing, but it is one of the most important tools a principal must master quickly. In particular, principals devote 80 percent of their time to interpersonal communication (Lunenburg and Ornstein 2000). Given that, you must be consistent with remarks and positions, as differences would remove personal trust and organizational consistency.

The principal's usual vehicle for formal communication within a school is a staff meeting. However, with the advent of technology, much of the "administrivia" previously shared in staff meetings can and should be communicated via e-mail. With the focus on improved academic performance measured through yearly tests, many school districts require professional development activities after the student day. To avoid taking up even more of a teacher's time, you will want to conduct shorter, more efficient staff meetings. Staff meetings are typically held at regular intervals throughout the year, in many schools once a month. The meetings offer the opportunity to address the staff as a whole and to address questions and concerns. The topics and efficiency of the meetings send strong signals to the staff.

One method to improve meetings is to establish ground rules (Brassard 1995). Plan the meeting and script your agenda in order for teachers to get in and out as quickly as possible. Keeping the meeting short will keep the teachers focused. As an example, the ground rules formulated by the Crystal Middle School staff have made meetings both professionally enriching and productive (Rogenski 1996). The middle school's model displayed here would be applicable to other typical meetings, such as department meetings, team meetings, and committee meetings.

Faculty Meeting Ground Rules

Agenda items

- All "information only" items should be distributed in writing.
- Times will be set and indicated for each presenter.
- Time will be allotted in the agenda for positive acknowledgment of staff members.

Time limitations

- Comments on issues and items will be limited to 1 to 2 minutes per person per turn.
- Limit discussion on agenda items to 15 minutes.
- Limit meetings to 1 hour and 20 minutes.

Discussion and comments

- Respond professionally and respectively. Stay focused on issues.
- Make your point brief and succinct.
- Comment only on items that pertain to the entire group.

If a new agenda item comes up, assign it to the next meeting with a presenter.

Assign a facilitator/monitor for rule enforcement.

Source: Rogenski, K. (1996). Control your staff meetings. *Thrust for Educational Leadership* 26(2), 14–17.

Brock and Grady (2004) advise new principals in the first year to be especially careful in communication because an event appearing to involve only one class or a small group of students may affect many others. Other important types of communications, for individuals and groups, inside and outside of the school, are the following written and electronically transmitted materials: "letters of commendation, personal notes, cards, daily bulletins, monthly newsletters, press releases to newspaper, and topic memoranda" (Lunenburg and Ornstein 2000, p. 200). With most schools using e-mail, teachers, auxiliary staff, cafeteria workers, and custodial staff should check at the end of each period for any new information coming from the administration. A well-informed staff is able to react quickly to any changes throughout the day by computer.

An integral part of any well-functioning organization is a set of guidelines or procedures standardizing and streamlining operations. By articulating in writing the year's expectations and goals, the principal documents what is expected of teachers. The staff handbook for the school includes information such as morning and afternoon duties, lunchroom assignments, dress code for teachers and students, weekly meetings, and evacuation procedures for fire and safe school audits. A handbook makes curriculum information such as dates for midterm reports, report cards, and grading scales readily accessible. From a principal's standpoint, written, established policies remove the need to reinvent the wheel, and, equally important today, protect the principal and the school from litigation both from within and outside the schoolhouse.

As principal, you will also need to develop the student handbook—written documentation of the rules governing student activities in school. You should include topics such as attendance, grading scales, dress codes, media services, computer-use permission forms, lunch detentions, and requirements for extracurricular activities. The smart school leader does not put anything in the handbook that the district cannot support. Of course, these should also be put on the school's Web site, and hard copies should be provided for those who request them.

Managing Resources

In a climate of scarce resources, as defined by constricted state and local budgets, the important mandate for an efficient school has become paramount. Only in highly unlikely circumstances will a principal encounter a school without the structural elements of an organizational chart, job descriptions, budgetary reports, daily checklists of duties, and so on. An effective school leader will be competent in these requirements. The key resources that an efficient principal has to draw upon to operate a school are district budget allocations, staff, technology, the building, business partnerships, and parents.

Fiscal resources. An important management tool is the school's nonpersonnel budget. Typically, less than five percent of the district's annual budget relates to daily operations and consumable goods. However, creating a budget as a whole-school endeavor enables you to reinforce the goals being aligned with the school mission and vision and offer real participation to the entire staff (Slosson 2000). In the report *Breaking Ranks*, researchers said budget decisions should be made at the school level to ensure that they meet the needs of the school (National Association of Secondary School Principals 1996).

Effective school programs should not be eliminated; therefore, school administrators must determine how to most effectively allocate the funding received. The first step toward competent spending is a thorough analysis of the school's needs and a vision statement that addresses those needs. The budget for a school is both an accounting system and a planning document for the year. As an accounting system, the budget is illustrated through a series of categories such as instruction, athletics, travel, staff development, or media. Some schools may have more extensive categories. Many principals increase leadership capacity by including the staff in budget deliberations. Budget priorities should be determined by the goals aligned with the school's mission and vision. There should be a direct link between the budget and the goals in order for the resources to be most effectively used to increase student achievement (Odden and Archibald 2000).

High school principal James Slosson includes school staff when creating the budget. This also allows the teachers and noninstructional personnel to realize exact costs related to the available funds. Slosson prepares spreadsheets communicating to all the stakeholders the amount of money available for items, how the money is spent, a history of spending for the year, and a guide for future spending. This helps teachers understand, for example, that if the copier paper runs out at year's end due to overuse, there will be no more monies to replenish the supply. Slosson recommends publishing the budget, goals, and final allocations for all stakeholders to review. "The rationale for the publication is the school community will operate more supportively if they understand where the money comes from, where it goes, and why it goes there" (Slosson 2000, p. 57).

Monies may come from a variety of sources—not just the district, but PTA fund-raisers, parent donations, athletic booster clubs, and contributions from businesses may supplement the district budget allocations. The entrepreneurial principal frequently finds ways to solicit sizeable amounts of monies from the community. Sometimes schools are given monies from the federal government for a specific purpose. The principal must keep a close eye on federal funding because of the potential of a federal audit, which could result in the loss of federal funds for a district.

Such a process is very important in light of a long-term trend identified by data collected by the National Center for Education Statistics (NCES) since 1920. The researchers report that the percentage of school disbursement allocations for instruction continually drops while the percentage for operations increases. Overall, resources are slow to rise in comparison to the demand for increased student/school performance (Picus 2000).

To address such challenges, the Committee on Economic Development recommends that districts allow principals more autonomy in the school's spending. The committee suggests setting goals for and monitoring student achievement, using state and national standards, and ensuring that adequate resources are provided to schools to meet such goals (Oswald 1995).

Within the school, the principal has several responsibilities of equal importance to allocating the budget. Sergiovanni (1990) suggests using the Planning Programming Budgeting System (PPBS). PPBS connects the creation of the budget to instruction. PPBS has the following requirements:

1. Conduct a needs assessment.

2. Evaluate existing goals.

3. Identify new goals.

4. Rank and weight all goals according to priority.

5. Assign goals to various programs and units.

6. Allocate monies to departments and units based on the importance of goals for which they are responsible.

As principal, you must ensure that the school's (or in many cases the district's) procedures for authorizing a commitment are known and followed. Reviewing the budget involves an administrative staff member and the principal reviewing the request and noting the amount spent to date versus the annual budgeted amount. Pardon the pun, but the "buck" really does stop at the principal's desk. If within budget and the request is demonstrably linked to the school's vision, mission, and goals, the principal should approve the request. Another important step involving budgets is the periodic sharing with stakeholders of expenditures versus the allocations. Keeping the staff informed reinforces the importance of efficiently managing scarce funds. A third element is making selective transfers among various accounts based on the tracking of expenditures and the changing needs (Ubben, Hughes, and Norris, 2001) of the school as related to the vision and school improvement plan.

Human resources. By far, the principal's most important resource—the school faculty and staff—is one that principals cannot always control fully, if at all. Generally, the number of staff members, teachers, and support staff is set by state and district ratios that dictate the number of teachers based on the number of students. Consequently, a principal must maximize effective and equitable instruction by carefully assigning teaching responsibilities, recruiting staff who will fit within the culture, and assigning students by need and learning styles rather than simply by numbers. This is a clear case of where equal treatment of unequal needs is not equal. Positive reinforcement for teachers who accept student assignments based on need rather than equal numbers is imperative.

Historically, we have seen parent volunteers and parent/teacher organizations as a major source of help for schools. Volunteers provide services such as tutoring, making copies, and grading papers. These tasks reduce what the school has to pay out; consequently, there are more funds for maintenance or other needs. Parent/teacher organizations have demonstrated abilities to raise funds via various means in order to purchase equipment, make capital improvements, and provide supplies. It would not be impractical to look to such organizations for projects such as refurbishing a bathroom, sprucing up the entrance area, redoing a gym floor, or reseeding the athletic fields.

Parent/teacher organizations and parent volunteers can be important resources for effective schools. Parent volunteers are able to serve as tutors for individual students and conduct mini-lessons for small groups of students. Additionally, volunteers may take on tasks such as grading papers, rounding up supplies, and cleaning up after lessons that free up teachers for concentrating on instructional activities.

Business partnerships with schools also offer similar benefits as a resource. Initially, such relationships revolved around monetary donations. That may no longer be the case for most schools; the relationship has evolved to genuine partnerships. Business partners now participate in mentoring students and teachers, tutoring, counseling, developing friendships with students, helping develop and strive toward the school's vision and goals, helping obtain equipment and resources, and offering team training. These relationships send the important message that people care about the schools and students and want them to be successful (Sammon and Becton 2001).

Senior citizens can be another valuable and free resource. Reach out to nearby senior social agencies and senior residential centers. Retirees are usually vigorous and healthy well into their eighth decade. They have skills and time that many of them would love to share with students. With today's extended families often literally living thousands of miles from loved ones, senior citizens in the schools can give and receive personal contacts needed and welcomed by both the students and the volunteers.

School facilities. To enhance the school's resources, a principal must enlist the staff and students into treating the facilities with positive regard, reinforcing behavior that keeps buildings and grounds clean and neat and that helps to eliminate destructive acts. You need to work with district facilities staff to prioritize and quantify maintenance needs and to lobby for those priorities. Finally, you can look to involve parent organizations, business partnerships, and charitable foundations as resources and advocates for the school's facility needs.

Effective schools strive for quality. However, providing quality education may be difficult without adequate resources. According to Stephen Covey (1991), "society wants education to handle all of its basic ills, its deeper problems" (p. 302). It is unlikely that this can happen and impossible without all the stakeholders working toward the same goals, mission, and vision. Robert Barkley, Jr., of the National Education Association asserts that schools must understand what the school needs are and then as a community agree and devote all of its resources to improvement of those needs (Oswald 1995).

Promoting a Safe Learning Environment

A critical responsibility of an administrator is the safety of the students. As principal, you must actively pursue school safety to ensure that the students are able to learn in a safe environment. Administrators must take proactive stances to develop schools where the organization, operations, and resources are directed to maintain environments conducive to learning. School safety is often thought of in terms of cameras, metal detectors, and other technology; however, school safety is much more than just hardware and security personnel.

The principal is the leader of a safe school organization. The school's principal must incorporate the necessary hierarchy of safety personnel. The initial step you should take is to create a safety committee of school community members. The committee's involvement is important because it presents different experiences and perspectives with regard to the school's safety needs (North Carolina Department of Juvenile Justice and Delinquency Prevention, n.d.). The role of the committee should be to determine the definition of what a safe school is, identify potential threats to the school's safety, and create a plan to make the school safe or safer (North Carolina Department of Juvenile Justice and Delinquency Prevention, n.d.).

Researchers state that school safety operations begin with assessing the school and establishing partnerships with law enforcement and emergency personnel (Trump 2002). The Center for the Prevention of School Violence has points to consider when the principal and the committee assess the school (North Carolina Department of Juvenile Justice and Delinquency Prevention, n.d.). The first recommendation from the Center's staff is to examine the facility. The safety team can follow the principles of school safety designed by the Crime Prevention Through Environmental Design (CPTED) (Blue 2000):

- Increase territorial concern.
- Improve the ability to observe the campus.
- Control access to the school's campus.

Students, school staff, and the school's community can help keep a watchful eye on the school as one way to increase territorial concern. For example, clearly identify entrances and specific school areas, such as the office, library, and so on. The school should make the entrances people are supposed to use inviting. Improve indoor and outdoor lighting if necessary, and keep school grounds clean and nicely landscaped. You might separate grade levels and other designated groupings, creating a school within a school (Blue 2000).

A resource that is commonly thought of in relation to safe schools is the school's resource officer (SRO) who acts as a law enforcement officer, law-related counselor, and law-related education teacher. The first responsibility of an SRO in a school is to keep the peace. According to a report from the National Association of School Resource Officers, the officers believe being present in schools is a deterrent to school violence (Kennedy 2002). The researchers reported that crime is reduced as the SRO develops positive relationships with students as well as all other school personnel. Other preventive tasks performed by SROs involved counseling students, chaperoning, coaching, classroom instruction, and presenting staff in-service programs (Trump 2002). In a survey of SROs, school security expert Kenneth S. Trump discovered that 90 percent of the 689 respondents stated that they had prevented 1 to 25 violent acts on a school campus from happening each year. Ninety-four percent reported that they have been able to intervene in a potential disruptive act as a result of student reporting (Gips 2002).

Resources many schools use to be safe are programs such as Students Against Destructive Decisions, conflict resolution programs, peer counseling, and self-esteem instruction. A three-year study conducted by Patti and Tobin (2001) looked at the implementation of a Resolving Conflict Creatively Program (RCCP). The goal of RCCP is to educate young people to express and handle themselves emotionally to practice conflict resolution in a nonthreatening manner and to admire diversity (Patti and Tobin 2001). The researchers revealed that a crucial ingredient to the program's success was the support the principal provided the students, the program, and the school.

Other resources relating to school safety include the fire and police departments, emergency medical services, and social services. These resources can provide expertise in assessment, planning, and practicing. Involvement of those resources increases the likelihood that in the event of a real situation, the student population will be safe from harm (North Carolina Department of Juvenile Justice and Delinquency Prevention, n.d.).

Violence is less likely to occur if there is a chance the perpetrator will be noticed. The second recommendation from the CPTED is to improve the visibility of the school's campus. Methods schools can incorporate in the school safety plan could include removing obstructions from inside and outside the building, keeping the interior and exterior of the school well lit, and positioning school employees to maximize visibility of the school's grounds (Blue 2000). Researchers state that a study of 377 elementary and middle school students in two urban areas found that the students did not feel safe in areas designated as "undefined" space (Astor, Meyer, and Pitner 2001, p. 519). In addition, they found that these were locations where there was no school supervision; therefore, the locations favor unsafe behavior such as bullying unless supervision is increased.

CPTED's final principle is control of the school's campus and access to it. Strategies include defining and clearly identifying parking areas, pedestrian areas, entrances, and exits. The school's landscape should be kept trimmed and low, avoiding dense foliage and opaque walls. The school should have a friendly but strict visitor policy with sign-in, sign-out sheets and badges. Within the building, there should be organized libraries and locker rooms to accommodate easy supervision (Blue 2000).

Unfortunately, today school safety is thought about in the context of school violence. However, safety also includes prevention planning for natural disasters and student and staff injuries. Every school needs to have planned procedures to handle fires, tornados, bomb threats, and student injuries. Not only must a plan exist, but it must be practiced periodically (North Carolina Department of Juvenile Justice and Delinquency Prevention, n.d.).

Student or staff injuries require reflex action as well. It is important that all school personnel know the staff members with first aid or cardiopulmonary resuscitation (CPR) training. These are an essential part of the principal's operations and should be included in the school's safety plan. Quinn (2002) presents the following recommended ingredients of a school's crisis plan:

- A list of crisis team members and their roles.
- A telephone tree of staff phone numbers to call in emergencies.
- A list of essential emergency numbers (police, fire, hospital, etc.).
- A list of personnel with special expertise (CPR, first aid, etc.).
- Emergency procedures (for intruders, bomb threats, etc.).
- A special code to alert team members.
- Staff schedules.
- A school map showing locations of bathrooms, phones, and exits.
- Sample letters (crisis announcements, condolences, etc.).
- Location of the school emergency supply kit, which should include a battery-powered bullhorn, first-aid kit, pagers or cell phones, a local phone directory, and a list of students with medical needs.
- An evaluation method to assess the plan's effectiveness.

Other suggestions offered by the Center for the Prevention of School Violence are to add to the school map utility, fire alarm, cable television, and sprinkler system shutoff, and computer and phone locations. The Center has additional school building information that is necessary to be on the list, such as aerial photos of the school, an evacuation plan, a procedure to cut off media and utility systems, and where to find keys to the school. Daily buses, attendance, staff, and student rosters should be in the safety kit, as well as student contact paperwork (North Carolina Department of Juvenile Justice and Delinquency Prevention, n.d.). All plans should be developed collaboratively among school personnel and community safety agencies such as the police and fire departments, local hospitals, and emergency management officials. All 50 states have similar plans and guidelines to follow. Learn these and be prepared!

Promoting an Efficient Learning Environment

The principal has a major responsibility in assuring that school business is conducted efficiently. That means clear and consistent communication, understanding of and compliance with policies and procedures, and sending and receiving ongoing feedback. Your role is to lead by expressing and acting upon the importance of these responsibilities and to provide moral and managerial oversight. The stakes are too high and the consequences too severe to proceed differently.

In today's society, rapid worldwide communication is commonplace. As principal, you must ensure that the school possesses the technology needed for the staff to use and instruct the students and to develop technology skills the students need to be competitive in the marketplace. Lunenburg and Ornstein (2000) state that in a quality school, the principal must have and use technology as a tool. This entails possessing and using the most recent forms of electronic devices available to stay on the cutting edge with regard to enhancing learning. Researchers have found that technology used in school's classrooms allows for more student-directed and student-centered learning. This results in positive learning environments and increased student achievement (National Association of Secondary School Principals 1996). Ubben, Hughes, and Norris (2001) add that principals and school improvement teams must incorporate technology in their overall plan for the immediate as well as future plans. They suggest possible topics for the technology improvement plan:

1. Technology integration into the curriculum.
2. Technology integration into school management.
3. Teacher, student, and staff training in technology utilization.
4. Expected student technology competencies.
5. Expected faculty and staff technology competencies.

In 2002, the International Society for Technology in Education spearheaded a collaborative effort among professional associations, state departments of education, and higher education faculty to develop Technology Standards for School Administrators (TSSA). We recommend that all school leaders become thoroughly familiar with these standards as technology becomes more dominant in school management and improvement in student achievement. Closely aligned with the ISLLC Standards, the TSSA more specifically define what school leaders need to know and be able to do in order to assure effective, efficient, and meaningful use of technology in the schools (International Society for Technology in Education 2002).

Promoting an Effective Learning Environment

The final segment of the matrix for ELCC and Standard 3 addresses the resources necessary to run an effective school. Accomplishing the tasks necessary to ensure an effective school requires important resources of training, time, and manpower.

School buildings are known to require a large amount of a district's resources to construct; however, due to the condition of most of America's schools, the buildings are generally not considered a resource. Logically, they are. Without a building to house students, it would be extremely difficult, if not impossible, to provide an effective education. A study of Washington, D.C., schools, along with other studies, relates the school building's condition to a direct effect on student learning. The studies found teachers feel better, the students and staff feel safer, and the instructional attitude is more positive in a school that is in good condition. In addition, buildings are being designed to enhance the delivery of education, creating a relationship between the building and the school's vision (Honeyman 1994).

One such example is Orem High School in Orem, Utah. The school is designed to accommodate more than academics. It is designed to be aesthetically pleasing to the students. The facility has many windows to let in natural light. There are spaces for the students to convene with classmates, and the school's colors replace the neutrality traditionally found in schools. Orem High School's design is based on the premise that it is important to create an environment that focuses on student learning, an environment where students are respected, and an environment where students want to be (Hansen and Childs 1998).

The Challenge

This chapter yields two major insights that are somewhat paradoxical. It is clear that a competent administrator must master a number of very diverse subjects. Yet it is also true that the one force that unifies and drives the organization to be successful is the innate leadership ability of the principal.

Implications for the leadership. School leadership requires knowledge and the ability to competently apply that knowledge. An effective leader must guide the school's members and the school's community toward an agreed-upon vision, mission, and goals. As a foundation for leadership, mutual trust must be created between the administrator and the stakeholders of the school. Principals must model team building, teamwork, and authentic shared decision making. An effective leader builds a school that involves the entire community, and everyone shares the rewards of a nurturing learning environment.

Implications for the faculty. ISLLC and ELCC Standards 3 provide a framework for the faculty of what to expect of the principal. The principal should ensure that the teachers are able to provide instruction in an environment that is safe. The principal should have plans in place in case of hazards as well as inform the school's members about the plans, and the plans should be practiced. Teachers should also expect the principal to supply the necessary resources and financial support needed to be effective educators. That may require the principal to seek resources from nontraditional sources. Teachers need to have the skills and equipment to effectively instruct the students on the latest technology. The principal should develop and implement staff development in any area that might be beneficial to the school. Finally, and most importantly, the faculty should expect the principal to be the unifying force of the school. This should be demonstrated through the principal's communication and actions.

Implications for student achievement. The students, staff, and parents should expect the principal to lead the school in a unified fashion toward a mutually developed and shared vision, mission, and goals. The teachers should provide students with classrooms that are safe learning environments, and the school as a whole should have preventive measures to protect the students from danger. The students should expect the principal to lead the faculty to provide them with a holistic education, which has adequately prepared them for either further education or the job market. The principal should ensure that the students not only develop academic skills but benefit from an education that prepares them to be productive members of a democratic society.

Implications for role of the principal. ISLLC and ELCC Standards 3 define the organizational, operational, and resource aspects of leading a school to be safe, efficient, and effective. The role of the principal requires solid knowledge about the following: safety procedures, requirements, plans, and resources; administrative processes needed to keep a school functioning, such as hiring and retaining teachers and other members of the school's staff; technology and the skills to use it; school financing and budgets; and how to most beneficially organize the school. Principals must be able to efficiently and effectively utilize this knowledge base with the available resources and be capable of leading others at the school to be effective. Principals must be resilient and demonstrate to the school's community that in spite of what may come their way, providing students with positive learning experiences in a safe and healthy environment will always be the first concern of the staff and principal.

Suggested Readings

Chance P. and E. Chance. 2002. *Introduction to Educational Leadership and Organizational Behavior.* Larchmont, NY: Eye On Education.

Davis, S., L. Darling-Hammond, M. LaPointe, and D. Meyerson, 2005. *School Leadership Study: Developing Successful Principals* (Review of Research). Stanford, CA: Stanford University, Stanford Educational Leadership Institute.

Levine, A. (2005). *Educating school leaders.* Washington, DC: The Education Schools Project.

Suggested Activities

1. Complete a brief reflection about the material in Chapter 3 in your reflection journal. Specifically, how do the essential knowledge and skills differ when comparing ISLLC to ELCC?

2. As a class, determine four or five technology standards that you feel need to be developed for future principals. In small groups, select one of these

standards and develop concrete strategies how these can be learned by your class. How would you use the knowledge learned from these standards in a school setting?

3. Review and critique an actual school safety plan. Present the product as a class report or in a written paper.

4. Select one book from a list given to you by your professor and critique. Prepare a brief paper (four to five pages) that includes an overview, information about the author, and the book's value to a school leader.

5. Using the case study *Zero Tolerance,* written by Dr. Stanley A. Schainker, participate in a whole-class discussion to list the major issues, stated and unstated, in the case. Then, in small groups, develop strategies to address the stated as well as unstated issues.

Zero Tolerance

by
Stanley A. Schainker, University of North Carolina at
Chapel Hill (with permission)

Jackie Lloyd, the first-year African-American assistant principal at the thousand-student Hilltop Middle School, has always believed that a zero-tolerance policy for fighting made sense. Now she isn't so sure. Hilltop has a long-standing policy that any student involved in a fight is automatically suspended for ten school days. Late yesterday afternoon Billy Wilson, an African-American eighth grader, came into her office and told her a group of black students had been hassling him for taking school seriously and trying "to show us all up" by getting good grades. He also reported that this same group threatened him "if he didn't stop playing the Man's game." Ms. Lloyd requested the names of the students involved, and Billy reluctantly supplied them. She told him not to worry because she would take care of everything the next morning and he would be protected while at school.

The following morning she instructed the dean of students to investigate Billy's concern. She also intended to caution Billy to stay away from any place in school that would bring him into contact with the group and to alert the teachers that there could be trouble. Unfortunately, she was unable to follow through on her plans, because another emergency took her attention for the entire morning.

At lunchtime, a fight broke out in the cafeteria between Billy and four of the boys from the group he had identified. At the time there were no teachers present in the cafeteria, even though three teachers had been assigned to that monitoring assignment. Witnesses confirmed that Billy told the other boys he did not want any trouble and had fought them only after he had been pushed, kicked, and hit at least twice by the instigators. The fight was eventually stopped by the security guard with help from two teachers who escorted all five youngsters to the office.

When Ms. Lloyd talked with Billy, he tearfully asked why she had not taken care of everything and protected him as she had promised. Feeling quite guilty, she tried to explain her hectic morning, but was not successful in convincing Billy. Then she informed him she would have to suspend him for ten days for fighting because that was the automatic consequence for any fight. Incredulous, Billy argued, "In the real world people get off all the time if they kill someone in self-defense when attacked. You mean in school, if you're attacked and try to defend yourself, you get the same punishment as the attackers? That doesn't make sense! It's stupid and unfair! Do you really think I'm as guilty as the other four guys? You know I'm not. I tried to handle this the right way by coming to you, and now you're going to punish me!"

The other four boys all admitted to Lloyd that they started the fight. She then went to the principal and explained the entire case to him, and requested leeway in the suspension decision. The principal responded, "C'mon, Jackie. Don't be such a bleeding heart. You know we have a zero-tolerance policy. Billy was fighting, so he gets suspended for ten days. It's as simple as that. If he is not suspended, we undermine the whole policy and tell all the students that they can get away with fighting. This will result in chaos. Suspend him and forget about it. He'll get over it."

But Jackie Lloyd could not forget about it. Poor Jackie. Poor Billy. Poor school.

MAJOR CHAPTER ASSIGNMENT

As two large groups, complete a team building staff plan for new principals using the design below. With your professor's permission, invite three first-year principals to join one group and three fifth-year principals to join the other group. Design your plans and then compare and discuss. Does more experience really matter?

Team building to develop a trusting environment: A model staff development plan for new principals	
Staff Development Activities	**Assessment/Demonstration of Knowledge**
In groups of four to five, address some segment of Standard 3, such as the development of a crisis plan.	The task is important, but the main purpose is the team-building process.
Develop a vision and mission statement for the team.	

Team building to develop a trusting environment *(continued)*	
Staff Development Activities	**Assessment/Demonstration of Knowledge**
Identify the stakeholders with regard to the assigned task.	Team trainer meets with team to discuss progress and difficulties: ◆ Communication (speaking, listening, and providing constructive feedback) ◆ Setting up ground rules ◆ Identifying expectations of and barriers to success ◆ Defining and assigning the team roles, planning additional meeting times and places ◆ Decision making
Identify expectations of and barriers to success.	
Develop an action plan.	
Collect, analyze, and interpret data.	
Present a report on the plan and findings at staff/faculty meeting.	
Reflect on the task as a team-building process.	Reflective journals.

Safe Schools and Standard 3

In the 1980s, inner city schools experienced numerous school shootings, which were largely ignored by the media. School shootings in middle America, however, were unheard of a few years ago, and even today they are rare. According to the FBI, "adolescent violence in general, and homicides in particular, have decreased since 1993" (O'Toole n.d., 2). Nevertheless, the sheer magnitude, senselessness, and violence of a school massacre amplify our insecurity, giving the impression that school violence is epidemic.

Unfortunately, with the major focus on serious and deadly violence, educators become numb to the thousand acts of "low-level" violence that occur in schools each week. Name-calling, shoving, vandalism, insults, schoolyard pranks, and other forms of bullying pale in comparison to the wanton shooting of students and teachers. With sensibilities dulled, it is tempting for principals to dismiss bullying as unpleasant but normal adolescent behavior and to chalk it up as "kids being kids." Such an attitude could prove deadly.

The Continuum of Violence

Bullying may be a catalyst for future delinquency and more extreme acts of school violence for both the bully and the student being bullied. A strong association between a student's environment, peer rejection, and exposure to aggression, either as perpetrator or victim, and future delinquency and violence is reported in a large body of research. When dealing with bullying, it may be useful to view bullying and violence on a continuum of behavior rather than as unrelated behaviors. At the low end of the continuum is bullying, which Espelage, Bosworth, and Simon (2000) define as "a set of behaviors that is 'intentional and causes physical and psychological harm to the recipient.' Bullying includes actions such as name-calling or teasing, social exclusion, and hitting" (p. 327), which now has evolved to the Internet and is known as *cyber bullying*. Unfortunately, bullying is rampant in our schools. Estimates from studies put the percentage of individuals being bullied as high as 30 percent. The authors have interviewed students and learned that the bullies are even getting bullied. The climate of a school can be affected by bullying behaviors if they go unchecked; threats and intimidation associated with bully behaviors can create a negative atmosphere for all students.

The National Association of Elementary School Principals (2003) reports that "one in 10 students is regularly harassed or attacked by bullies [and] 15 percent of all schoolchildren are involved in bully/victim problems" (p. 1).

A school environment that permits bullying to go unchecked is one that may be inviting more extreme violence. Citing Albert Bandura's social learning theory, Espelage, Bosworth, and Simon (2000) note:

> The external environment contributes, in large part, to acquiring and maintaining aggression. Children learn from role models, including adults and peers, to use aggressive means to achieve their goals. [Moreover], the relationship between early aggression [bullying], peer rejection, and exposure to violence . . . and later violence is strong. The author found that students who bully were themselves at an increased risk of being physically abusive and of having a criminal record as adults. (p. 328)

"It is difficult to find any other childhood factor," writes Huesmann, "that predicts more of the variation in adult aggression than does childhood aggression" (Huesmann and Guerra 1997, p. 408). Echoing similar findings, Arsenio, Cooperman, and Lover (2000) argue: "Beginning in the preschool years, childhood aggression is an important predictor of difficulties in social functioning and adjustment" (p. 438). Ladd and Profilet (1996) have found that "Children's use of aggression . . . consistently emerges as one of the best predictors of later maladaptation. . . . aggressive behavioral styles are predictive of peer rejection . . . and children who display aggressive tendencies . . . appear to be at greater risk for adjustment problems in early adolescence" (pp. 1008–1009).

Likewise, Stattin and Magnusson (1989) observed that when "compared with low and normally aggressive subjects, the early high aggressive subjects . . . were involved in more serious crimes [and] . . . were particularly more likely to engage in confrontative and destructive offenses" (p. 718). Summarizing a large body of research on the relationship between peer relationships and aggressive behavior, Newcomb, Bukowski, and Pattee (1993) concluded: "A clear consensus exists among social developmental researchers that children's peer relations provide unique and essential contributions to social and emotional development . . . . rejected children were found to be more aggressive" (pp. 99, 114–115).

Although researchers show a strong association between peer rejection and exposure to aggression and future delinquency and violence, it is a large leap from bullying to the kind of violence exhibited at Columbine. Clearly, the overwhelming majority of students who bully, or who are bullied, never become killers. Nevertheless, the connection between aggression, peer rejection, and later violence suggests that low-intensity violence or aggression can lead to tragic cases of extreme school violence.

Training Our Children to Kill

Grossman (2000/2001) provides helpful insight into how repeated participation in or exposure to violence can lead to desensitization and to extreme violence. A former Army Ranger and paratrooper, Lt. Col. Dave Grossman is an eminent authority on the subject of motivating killers. Grossman asserts that "killing does not come naturally; you have to be taught to kill. . . . Killing requires training because there is a built-in aversion to killing one's own kind" (p. 40). To buttress his argument, Grossman cites military statistics showing that before the Vietnam War only 15 to 20 percent of individual riflemen could bring themselves to kill. This obviously presented a problem for the military, which it set out to solve. "By Vietnam," writes Grossman, "the [killing] rate rose to over 90 percent. The method in this madness: desensitization" (p. 42).

The process of desensitization, the frog in the kettle syndrome, is fundamental to understanding the relationship between early childhood violence in the form of bullying and later violence. As Grossman puts it:

> How the military increases the killing rate of soldiers in combat is instructive because our culture today is doing the same thing to our children. The training methods militaries use are brutalization, classical conditioning, operant conditions, and role modeling. . . . Brutalization and desensitization are what happens at boot camp. . . . Something similar to this desensitization toward violence is happening to our children through violence in the media. . . . *The Journal of the American Medical Association* published the definitive epidemiological study on the impact of TV violence. . . . In every nation, region, or city with television, there is an immediate explosion of violence on the playground, and within 15 years there is a doubling of the murder rate. Why 15 years? That is how long it takes for the brutalization of a three- to five-year-old to reach the "prime crime age." (pp. 42–43)

Although Grossman (2000/2001) is addressing the impact of violence in the media on violence among adolescents, a parallel can be drawn with witnessing, participating in, or being victimized by constant bullying. Potentially, the perpetrator becomes progressively desensitized to violence. A bully who receives reinforcement (classical conditioning) in the form of acceptance from a subgroup of peers, experiences no negative reinforcement through school discipline, and has been conditioned (like the vast majority of our students) by sustained exposure to the pervasive violence in the media may come to associate violence with pleasure. In a chilling example of classical conditioning that desensitizes our students to violence, Grossman recounted the reaction of students to the Jonesboro shootings:

> Our children watch vivid pictures of human suffering and death, and they learn to associate it with their favorite soft drink and candy bar, or their girlfriend's perfume. After the Jonesboro shootings, one of the high-school teachers told me how her students reacted when she told them about the shootings at the middle school. "They laughed," she told me with dismay. A similar reaction happens all the time in movie theaters when there is bloody violence. The young people laugh and cheer and keep right on eating popcorn and drinking pop. We have raised a generation of barbarians who have learned to associate violence with pleasure, like the Romans cheering and snacking as the Christians were slaughtered in the Coliseum. (p. 43)

Is this stretching the association between bullying and school shootings too far? Not according to the Exceptional Case Study Project (ECSP) report released by the U.S. Secret Service (USSS), the goal of which was to analyze information about the behavior and thinking of young persons who commit acts of targeted violence in our nation's schools. According to the report authored by Vossekuil, Reddy, and Fein (2000), a relationship exists between bullying and extreme targeted school violence. "Targeted violence at school is rarely impulsive; the attacks are typically the end result [sic] of an understandable and often discernible process of thinking and behavior . . . *In a number of cases, having been bullied played a key role in the attack* [emphasis added]" (pp. 2–3). Vossekuil, Reddy, and Fein go on to observe:

> In over ⅔ of the cases, the attackers felt persecuted, bullied, threatened, attacked, or injured by others prior to the incident. A number of attackers had experienced bullying and harassment that was longstanding and severe. *In those cases, the experience of bullying appeared to play a major role in motivating the attack at school* [emphasis added]. (p. 7)

Maslow's theory of human motivation may shed light on why bullying may trigger a violent attack. According to Maslow (1973), human beings are motivated to satisfy their needs, which are "organized into a hierarchy of relative prepotency" (p. 157). Human motivation begins with physiological needs, followed by the need for safety, love, and self-esteem, culminating with the need for self-actualization. Each need emerges and becomes more important in human motivation as lower needs are progressively satisfied. When a basic need is unmet, however, it can become an all-consuming preoccupation. The result, according to Maslow, is that "the [individual's] whole philosophy of the future tends also to change" (p. 156). In other words, the unmet need becomes the central organizing principle for behavior and the cognitive framework for interpreting the world. Everything is interpreted in terms of satisfying the unmet need. All other concerns are subordinated to meeting this need.

The need for safety, the second most fundamental need in Maslow's hierarchy, is of particular relevance to a discussion of school violence. Every student has an intrinsic need to feel safe. Persistent bullying, which threatens a student's physical, social, and psychological safety, may trigger an emergency response in the form of violence.

The bullied student, whose safety, love, and self-esteem needs are relentlessly threatened, may lash out against all perceived perpetrators or co-conspirators. Like a cornered animal, the student victimized by bullying may see violence as the only means of self-protection.

What Principals Must Do

The place to begin is by taking bullying and other forms of student-to-student harassment seriously. Bullying is not child's play. The research is clear; there is a strong association between peer rejection, exposure to violence, bullying, and future delinquency and school violence.

Begin by establishing a school culture that will not tolerate any form of harassment. Principals should establish clear expectations and sanctions and communicate those to the school community, beginning with students. Teachers and students should be taught to take even small acts of unkindness, verbal abuse, or any other form of harassment or bullying seriously. By focusing on small, seemingly insignificant acts of unkindness and bullying, principals and teachers set an expectation and standard for interpersonal relationships and conflict resolution.

Second, establish a social relations training program. In a study designed to measure the effectiveness of comprehensive social relations intervention programs in reducing aggressive behavior among children, Lochman et al. (1993) found "significant reductions in aggression and social rejection and improvements in peer prosocial behavior." The authors noted that the findings are of particular importance "because it is the aggressive, rejected subgroup of children that is at the greatest risk for negative adolescent outcomes. Thus, the children most in need of intervention were those who were significantly affected by this social relations program" (p. 1057). The program suggested by Lochman et al. consists of four components: (1) social problem solving; (2) positive play training; (3) group-entry skill training; and (4) dealing effectively with strong negative feelings. For more detailed information, see Lochman et al. (1993).

Third, take character education seriously and infuse it throughout the school's culture and curriculum. Character education is not a separate course; it is the sum total of school culture, of what is taught in the classroom as right and wrong, of the rewards and sanctions given for certain behaviors, and of what teachers and principals model. In other words, we should strive to create schools that have a civilizing effect on our students. Writing of the civilizing influence of education, Plato asserted that "education . . . will have the greatest tendency to civilize and humanize [students] in *their relations to one another* [italics added], and to those who are under their protection" (Plato, p. 126). Although school principals cannot control the socialization that children receive outside of school, they can ensure that the school environment is one that tends to civilize rather than to corrupt students.

Children have a natural proclivity toward egocentrism, crudeness, defiance of authority, and aggression. If not corrected and restrained by the socializing and civilizing affects of parental guidance, social pressure, and good schooling, today's schoolyard bullying can become tomorrow's schoolyard shooting.

If we are to avoid another Jonesboro or Columbine, a great deal of effort must be exerted to cultivate the character of our students. Unfortunately, the soaring rates of violence in our schools and community demonstrate that we are failing. Too often, we teach our students how to make a decent living but not how to live decently. We teach them how to make babies but not how to create stable families. We teach them how to build companies but not how to build a good civilization. We teach them how to negotiate the deal but not how to negotiate interpersonal conflict. We teach them how to dress for success but leave them morally naked.

Placing Plato's sentiments in contemporary terms, sociologist James Wilson argued over a decade ago that "morality is innate . . . rooted in the very qualities that enable us to succeed as social animals . . . [however, our] moral sense is fragile . . . subject to buffeting by more elemental instincts—survival, greed, passion—but persistent nonetheless, very much like our sense of beauty" (Klein 1993, p. 1). Unfortunately, our moral sensibilities have been buffeted by the ascendancy of moral relativism, which forced character education in our schools underground. Advocates for moral education, including teachers and principals, are assumed to be motivated by religious fundamentalism or are dismissed as intellectual Neanderthals captivated by archaic notions of morality. "It is difficult," writes Wilson, "to say what effects have followed [our] effort to talk ourselves out of having a moral sense . . . we may have harmed vulnerable children who ought to have received surer guidance from family and neighborhood; we may have promoted self-indulgence when we thought we were endorsing freedom" (Klein, p. 1).

Our failure to produce morally literate children has made our children and us prisoners. We have become prisoners of fear, living in gilded homes behind locked doors and security systems. In too many instances, our schools have ceased to be open communities of learning. Instead, they increasingly resemble miniature prisons with locked doors, metal detectors, surveillance cameras, and guards roaming the halls to keep the "inmates" under control.

Fourth, take concrete steps to reduce the incidences of bullying. Hazler (1994, pp. 39–40) suggests several steps that principals can take:

1. *Don't look the other way.* Recognize bullying as a serious problem.

2. *Deal directly with the problem and take action immediately.*

3. *Get parents involved.* Let your students' parents know that you won't tolerate harassment of any kind.

4. *Create appropriate activities.* For example, use awareness activities to help your students focus on understanding how victims, bullies, and witnesses feel and why they act the way they do.

5. *Help teachers develop a classroom action plan.* Have the students agree on specific things they can do to lessen the problems in their class or at the school.

6. *Hold regular discussion with your students.* Try discussing examples of bullying from history and current events in class.

7. *Teach cooperation.* Encourage group work.

8. *Provide professional counseling when needed.*

Suggested Activities *(continued)*

6. Do you agree with this conclusion? Why or why not?

The schoolyard bully and the school shooter have one thing in common: they both act violently. Although bullying is on the lower end of this continuum of violence and shooting is on the extreme end, they are both engaged in the same act: inflicting harm and injury on others.

INDIVIDUAL OR CLASS REACTION

Some educators believe that this continuum of violence—teasing, harassment, and bullying—is associated with more extreme school violence. Consequently, school leaders must take bullying seriously and adopt a zero-tolerance policy for all forms of harassment.

Do you agree with the above reasoning? Why or why not? Defend your position from a research and a practical point of view.

---

7. Group Project

The class should be divided into three groups, one each for elementary, middle, and senior high schools. From examining ISLLC and ELCC Standards 3, make a list of the items the group thinks should be in each safe school plan. After this task is completed, visit state DPI Web sites and review actual school plans from your area. How close were you to including all of the requirements by your state?

4

Standard Four:
Collaboration as an Essential
of Leadership Development

*Coming together is a beginning; keeping together is progress;
working together is success.*

—Henry Ford

ISLLC Standard 4	ELCC Standard 4
A school administrator is an educational leader who promotes the success of all students by collaborating with families and community members, responding to diverse community interests and needs, and mobilizing community resources.	*Candidates who complete the program are educational leaders who have the knowledge and ability to promote the success of all students by collaborating with families and other community members, responding to diverse community interests and needs, and mobilizing community resources.*

The preparation of students for living during the 21st century depends on enrichment other than simply what is provided in the classroom. While schools have traditionally been the primary venue for educating students, educators have now assumed greater responsibility for moral and ethical development, crime and drug prevention, health and wellness, personal and interpersonal skills, and civic and social responsibility. Because educators have undertaken such a broad and evolving role, the need for increased parental involvement and community relations has come to the forefront.

Attainment of ISSLC and ELCC Standards 4 requires school leaders to take full advantage of their position to promote the relationship among the school, the parents, and the broader community. In order to do this, the school leader must have knowledge and understanding of the dynamics of the school community, be committed to collaboration and communication with those outside the school building, and have an appreciation for the value that diversity can bring to the school. Additionally, the principal must develop clear strategies and sound programs that are systematic, comprehensive, and ongoing. It is clear that the school leader must set the tone, expectations, and meaning for an effective school community relations plan.

In order to achieve the best possible education for students, educators must be actively and continuously involved with school–community relationships. The increasingly diverse nature of society should not only be acknowledged and respected but also treated as positive and constructive in the partnership. Regardless of differing opinions and perceptions, the relationships that schools establish with those outside the walls of the school must be rooted in mutuality and cooperation. The school leader is the role model in developing and nurturing these mutually supportive partnerships. The principal must make school–community relations a priority and show leadership in the process of creating and maintaining effective ties with parents and community members. School leaders are charged with working to generate more involvement and stimulating interest and sharing responsibility in creating better schools for children.

In this chapter, we summarize literature on school–community relations and offer various strategies and models for facilitating an effective plan. New and continuing principals can use the information in this chapter to gain insight about the importance of involving all stakeholder groups in the educational process as well as suggestions on how to do it effectively.

School leaders can also use concepts from this chapter to build goodwill and morale in the school. While our aim is to show how the internal public of the school impacts and influences parents and the community, much of what we offer is simply good practice in creating a positive and efficient climate in the school. New and continuing principals can use this chapter to improve shared decision making, communication, and efficiency with the internal public of the school.

The overall purpose of parental and community collaboration is to promote student success. Strong partnerships can support and advance student achievement. Principals can use this chapter to create and implement a school community relations plan that is centered around student achievement.

Educators are increasingly realizing that schools by themselves cannot provide all the skills and knowledge that students need to persevere and prosper in the new millennium. Communal and parental involvement in the educational process offers many benefits to both the educator and the learner. While the success of children is the primary motive for soliciting involvement from parents and the community, there are various other reasons for developing school, family, and community partnerships. Ultimately, these relationships will serve to improve school programs and school climate, increase parents' skills and leadership, connect families with others in the school and the community, provide additional support, and assist educators with their obligations. When there is a shared interest and responsibility for children, the potential for all involved is maximized.

Despite the obvious advantages, establishing and maintaining school partnerships with families and community groups is not always easily accomplished. Changing demographics bring to society ethnic diversity along with a variety of different belief systems, attitudes, and lifestyles. There have also been dramatic changes in family composition and arrangement. Additionally, socioeconomic status and social standing continue to stratify society. The diverse nature of society can complicate school, family, and community partnerships because expectations and demands may be contradictory. Various individuals and groups may have widely differing perceptions of the roles they play in making schools better places for children.

Even though diversity will present certain challenges, schools cannot exist isolated from the society to be served. As education becomes even more important, its methods more diverse, and its purposes more complex, educators must seek to intimately involve parents and other community members and groups. The school principal is in a good position to coordinate the efforts to build these relationships. Effective principals recognize the importance of developing and maintaining partnerships with parents and community groups. In essence, this involvement will enrich educational offerings and establish an important support base for the school.

While this chapter provides specific information that will guide school leaders in developing an ongoing, comprehensive school community relations plan, we also encourage school leaders to seek additional professional learning experiences in this area.

The Principal and Collaboration

As the principal, be versatile and open-minded. Endeavor to develop the skills and talents around you as you collaboratively work through processes to realize changes in the school. The vision for the school should include collaborative decision making, with all stakeholders including the school community of parents, students, and staff. Strive to develop an attitude of nurturing the learning community that supports the growth and development of individuals who have shared responsibilities for the success of the school.

Further, learn about the psychology that prevails among your students and families. Understand that the relationship between parent and child does not end when the student comes to school. As instructional leader, you will seek to incorporate this parental bond, together with the pushes and pulls from school and the community, into your vision of student learning.

"The research is quite clear on the effectiveness of parent and community involvement: in programs with a strong component of parent involvement, students are consistently better achievers than in otherwise identical programs with less parent involvement. In addition, students in schools that maintain frequent contact with their communities outperform those in other schools" (Sonia Nieto 2000).

Parental Participation in the School Environment

The school leader must actively devise strategies that encourage parental participation. School leaders should not leave it up to parents and families to take the initiative. Once the partnership is born, the school and the home can share responsibility for a student's learning. The relationship that results must be based on mutual respect and acknowledgment of the assets and expertise of each member. Schools should provide guidance in terms of the courses, grading procedures, and other pertinent facts that will make the transition from home environment to school environment easy. As instructional leader, take extra care not to make collaboration with parents a one-way communication. For instance, contacting parents when their child is in trouble and initiating parent–teacher conferences allow parents to become involved in their child's education, but they still represent a one-way highway of communicating. Collaboration instead must integrate strategies about how parents can help improve school programs or contribute to making the school environment a safe place for all students. Parents should be invited and encouraged to be involved in well-organized and coordinated social, academic, and personal issues that are so prevalent in a school setting today.

There are roadblocks that may prevent parents themselves from getting more and more active in their child's school. In the 21st century, students, especially those at the high school level, prefer their parents to be both less visible and less active in their schools. They may discourage their parents from volunteering or even participating in parent–teacher conferences. Keep this in mind, but do not let it deter you from actively engaging families in decisions on curriculum and instruction. You can also formulate tactics that involve parents in student-mediated conferences about coursework, academic progress, achievement, school safety, school discipline, and many other factors that may impact their school.

School leaders can choose among several innovative techniques to win parental support. Holding town meetings and hosting dinner at the school site provide venues for discussing issues and sharing information. Stay in touch through informal talk, printed announcements, word of mouth, telephone calls, or parent–teacher conferences. Enlist the services of other school personnel to serve as liaisons between the school and family. For example, the school nurse can make home visits, or designated school counselors can visit a student's home when that student stops coming to school. These home visits allow you to better understand the needs of families and how the school can help. Open school facilities to programs such as GED, adult literacy programs, or parental meetings where parents can give input about student and school progress.

Before the school year opens, solicit parent volunteers by sending home invitations and the necessary paperwork for parents to become actively involved in school affairs. This will open a forum that allows input for goal improvement and enable school staff and parents to formulate specific activities required to help all students meet challenging standards.

Principals need to reach out to parents, both those who are visibly active and those who basically remain in the background. One effective technique is the old-fashioned kaffeeklatsch. Such an event should be held in the community to help participants feel a little more comfortable. You might plan to convene a kaffeeklatsch every two or three weeks throughout the school year. Ask a family from the school to host the event, inviting friends and neighbors to their home for an informal discussion about the school and other education issues around the state or nation. Set aside two hours for the event, with the hosts providing coffee and juice and light snacks. The only topic off limits is personnel issues; this should never be a forum for attacking a school employee. The principal should lead the discussion, take brief notes, and follow up on any items that warrant further attention. Upon returning to your office, add the names of participants and hosts to a cumulative roster so you can spread invitations more broadly in the community. The openness of these kaffeeklatsches will do much to enhance positive perceptions of the school.

It is also critical that educators become well versed about what exactly is meant by parental involvement. As Marianne Bloch and Robert Tabachnick (1994) best put it, some see the roles of parents and teachers as distinct, with little overlap, while other parents believe there should be more shared visions, communication, or collaboration between teachers and parents over the education of their children. As school leader, you must be particularly sensitive to the diverse needs and perceptions of parents. Foster innovative techniques that encompass teacher conferences, bake sales, and extracurricular activities such as sports (Delgado-Gaitan 1990; Pink and Borman 1994). Plainly put, the decision making must not be unilateral; rather, it should be shared responsibility when addressing areas of implementation and school change as written in the school's vision. Be careful not to set up a competition between school and parents; instead, the relationship should be one of collaboration.

Teacher Involvement with the Family and Community

The responsibility for collaboration with parents should not rest solely on the principal. Other school personnel should be trained and equipped to promote and support family involvement. As school leader, take advantage of professional development on how to get productive family engagement in the school's affairs. Programs should address such issues as how best to:

- ◆ Develop parental skills.
- ◆ Communicate with families about school programs and student progress.
- ◆ Help families reinforce learning at home.
- ◆ Help families become active in the decision process.
- ◆ Coordinate community contributions and resources.
- ◆ Give teachers common planning or release time so that they can have time to work effectively with parents.

Instructional curriculum and accountability are vital for the success of any school. As instructional leader, you will want to ensure that parents know what students need to learn and at what levels of proficiency. Provide guidance so that parents have a better idea of what to do in the event their child is not performing to expectations. In particular, set forth the standards that govern the curriculum in an easily understood format so that parents can know how best to implement their own strategies at home. For example, your school might establish a community center where both parents and students can go to check out materials to enhance their own knowledge, or teachers can meet with parents and students to demonstrate the skills required for success in their classroom.

Instructional leaders should incorporate collaboration and communication into their vision not as ends in themselves, but as important processes spreading instructional improvement throughout their schools. For this community involvement to be viable, collaboration among the faculty must not be overlooked. In conjunction with the instructional leader, teachers and other staff personnel should be collaborative and have constant communication in order to understand different levels of the design about how to effectively involve the community. Principals must certainly "win" the house first, get widespread staff support for community involvement, then use strategies to involve the community. Failure to get this staff support will undoubtedly torpedo the whole process.

Even teachers who understand the importance of parental and community involvement may lack the knowledge and skills needed to effectively and efficiently include other adults in their classroom activities. This can represent a major barrier to school–community relations. As school leader, you can offer them ideas and strategies for soliciting support. Take advantage of staff development opportunities to guide teachers as they adopt the school community relations plan. Part of your job as principal is to hold teachers accountable for their role in the school community relations plan and follow up to ensure that they engage external stakeholders in a way that enhances teaching and learning (Barclay and Boone 1995)

Community Resources

Palmer (1998) states that we must ask, "What community resources can we tap to benefit our students?" Available resources can range from financial support by area businesses to community volunteers from local civic organizations. Universities or colleges can also offer resources to the local public schools in a variety of ways, ranging from providing tutoring services to students to providing staff development for teachers. As school leader, it is your responsibility to locate these resources and utilize them in a way that meets the needs of your students. Keep in mind that the school you lead is not packed and sealed in a vacuum. Rather, it exists within the context of several complex geographic entities, from the nation to the state, the school system, and the local system. From all of these geographic areas, the local community plays a key role in the success of the school.

In order to access community resources, establishing an effective relationship with the members of the community is necessary. Di Benedetto and Wilson (2004) contend that in establishing this relationship, a principal should develop a strategy first for school–community relations, taking into account the community's values and power hierarchy. By understanding the community at large, you can better identify potential areas of partnership as well as conflict. You can then find the ways that best involve the community in the school. It is also important that school leaders take part in civic activities outside the school in order to build positive school–community relations (Di Benedetto and Wilson).

To create and establish effective relationships with the school's external stakeholders, the dynamics of the community must be understood and both internal and external stakeholders must believe that diversity will enrich the educational process. School leaders must be dedicated to overcoming barriers that hinder communication and collaboration and work to involve parents, families, community organizations, and other community members to advance learning and teaching and to assist in the cognitive, social, emotional, and moral development of students.

The vision set forth as instructional leader must recognize that students in your domain bring more than educational needs into the classroom setting. In essence, this vision must incorporate other methods and tactics that will strongly enhance a student's learning. One such component draws on community support systems that recognize all aspects of a "whole child"—such as their health, family, and community—and provide interrelated human services to help the child become productive in later years. Principals should strive for services that are comprehensive and effective, maximizing the potential of community influence. School leaders need to seek out and work closely with frontline workers—community service workers, social workers, health workers, and others—to support their efforts with students and their families. Again, strive for continued interagency collaboration directed mostly to meeting the student and family needs.

School leaders must also be very careful in their selection of partnerships in the community. Look for and partner with organizations whose strong collaborative effort will improve student performance in school while at the same time reducing the student's chances of unemployment, delinquency, or adolescent pregnancy, to name a few prime hazards. Do not rely on a one-program dimension or programs that are destructive to the school goals. Rather, the programs must cumulatively have a positive impact on the student.

Community agencies play a critical role as catalysts for change, and the instructional leader must be aware of this. Continuously ask questions about whether the current program implementing the school's vision needs improvement and what role these agencies should play. Look at the students' educational performance and ascertain how well the school connects with these community service organizations. Keep the lines of communication open to encourage individual community groups to examine the current practices in schools and find ways to improve on them.

Marketing Strategies and Processes

Schools face ever-increasing competition for their services. Voucher programs and the push for school choice have helped to drive this competition in recent years. As parents gain access to more and more options, such as charter schools, private schools, parochial schools, and even home schooling, principals will find themselves having to market their schools to the community. Robenstine (2000) identifies several areas in which principals can make their schools more attractive to the general public. These strategies include being responsive to the customer (parents and students), attaining a competitive edge over other schools, and managing the budget efficiently and cost effectively. It will also be necessary for school leaders to be media savvy—to understand how to work with the local media so that the community sees the school at its best.

Decision Making

The responsibility to coordinate school affairs rests primarily with the principal. Today's greater empowerment of principals to run their schools adds to their responsibilities, but also allows them to include other stakeholders in the decision-making process. It is only through this collaborative effort that schools will begin to realize greater success. Yanitski (1997) stated that there were two types of stakeholders—legitimate and nonlegitimate groups. When making decisions, the principal must not neglect invaluable stakeholders such as teachers, parents, students, and other members of the community. Owens (1995) argues that principals—influenced, more often than not, by their desire to run a successful school—may be enticed to decide whether to make decisions alone or whether to involve the organization. The decision that eventually comes from the principal must reflect the needs of the school and community. It is important to note that according to Owens (1995), the decisions that principals ultimately make are irrelevant, whereas the "behavior" of the stakeholders is paramount to the success of the school.

Of course, some decisions are appropriately unilateral. The "boss" should not pause to consult with the faculty before deciding to evacuate the school in the case of a fire. Decisions to revise the curriculum, on the other hand, need to be discussed with the relevant stakeholders in the school: teachers, parents, and possibly even students. As a principal, guidelines will need to be developed and adhered to on how to best make decisions for the school while giving those within it a voice.

A Brief Review

In their annual *Phi Delta Kappan* Gallup Poll of the public's attitude toward public schools, the majority of respondents assigned either an A or a B to the schools in their communities. While giving schools these relatively high marks, 81 percent of those polled believed that a high percentage of students are under-achieving. Interestingly, the majority of respondents believed that parents are the most important factor in determining whether students learn in schools (Rose and Gallup, 2006). Most experts agree that parental involvement can be crucial to children's success in school.

Researchers from the U.S. Office of Educational Research and Improvement (1995) found that involving parents in the education of their children improves grades, standardized test scores, cognitive skills, and attendance. Additionally, when parents and families help elementary school children with their homework, social class and the parent's level of education become far less important factors in predicting the child's academic success. Epstein (1995) indicated that schools in which parents are highly involved and well informed are more likely to be very effective schools. The authors also contend that it is impossible to have a school that is excellent academically but ignores families and parents in the process.

Despite the obvious benefits, researchers have also reported different degrees and types of parental involvement depending on race, ethnicity, and socioeconomic status (Fan and Chen, 2001). Affluent families currently have more positive family involvement in comparison to economically disadvantaged families. In 1994, the Southern Regional Educational Board indicated that minority and limited English–proficient parents face many barriers when they attempt to collaborate with schools. These include lack of time and energy, language barriers, feelings of insecurity and low self-esteem, lack of understanding about the structure of the school and accepted communication channels, cultural incongruity, race and class biases on the part of school personnel, and perceived lack of welcome by teachers and administrators. Regardless of this, researchers agree that all parents want their children to be motivated to learn, to master basic academic skills, and to be socially competent. Even though parents may differ in their understanding of what it takes to achieve, they all want their children to be successful in school (Epstein 1995).

While families and schools have traditionally been viewed as having the greatest impact on the development of children, community involvement has also been deemed important in ensuring the success of children. Sanders (2001) defines school–community partnerships as the connections between schools and community individuals, organizations, and businesses, combined to promote students' social, emotional, physical, and intellectual development. Heath and McLaughlin (1987) argue that community involvement is important because "the problems of educational achievement and academic success demand resources beyond the scope of the school and of most families" (579). The authors claim that the demographic, cultural, and economic shifts in society account for why schools and families alone cannot provide sufficient resources.

A few researchers indicate that when community-based programs are involved, schools, parents, and students reap the benefits. Epstein (2001) shares a similar point of view by maintaining that community-based programs that are connected to schools are more likely to assist parents and increase student achievement and learning. Sanders (2001) found that one-on-one tutoring programs have caused an improvement in student grades and attendance. Epstein also stated that school–community collaborations enhance students' attitudes as well as the attitudes of parents and teachers. Additionally, Epstein contends that well-organized community-based programs can help educators to understand students' families, cultures, and customs. Toffler and Toffler (1995) posit that community collaboration is an effective way to provide a caring component to today's often-large assembly line schools.

In spite of the clear advantages that school–community partnerships bring to everyone involved, Sanders (2001) has identified several obstacles that prevent these relationships from forming. These barriers include the educators' fear of public scrutiny, staff burnout, teachers and administrators' perceptions that communities are uncaring or deprived of resources that contribute to the success of students, territorialism, the inability to assist all families in identifying the community programs that meet their needs, and the lack of reciprocity or two-way communication and collaboration.

Undoubtedly, parents and other members and groups from the community should be actively engaged in the educational process. Individual school-based autonomy will no longer be effective given the increasing diversity and complexity of today's society. The strongest support base for schools is the people that comprise the school community. As outlined in the ISLLC standards, school principals must be able to communicate and collaborate with the community and families of children in order to be effective in promoting the success of students (Council of Chief State School Officers 1996).

Essential Elements of Community Collaboration for School Leaders (ELCC)

Given the standards established in ISLLC and ELCC and the solid base of experts that support the joint efforts of parents and community in the educational process, it is clear that school leaders must extend efforts outside of the school building. The school principal alone is the most critical factor in determining the extent of parental and community involvement in the school. Successful collaboration requires the leadership of a knowledgeable and committed building principal. School leaders hold the key to convincing skeptics that community and parental programs can have a positive academic, social, emotional, and moral impact on students. The school principal must be fully aware and involved in the total support system for the school.

Assessing Perceptions

In order to take progressive actions toward parental and community collaboration, school leaders must first have the initial desire and interest. It is critical that educators examine their own current beliefs regarding involvement. Principals should reflect on answers to the following questions:

1. Should parents be recognized as the most important teachers of their children?

2. Does school leadership in the building play a major role in parent/community involvement?

3. Do parents have the right to be involved in some aspect of decision making for their child and in the school?

4. Do teachers have a responsibility to encourage input from families and community agents and to help parents become better teachers of their children?

5. Do parents really want to be involved or do they want to take over the school?

6. Does community and family involvement make success for the child easier?

7. Should schools actively encourage frequent, open, and two-way home–school communications?

8. Do most parents want the school to tell them how they can help their child at home? (Barclay and Boone 1995, p. 2)

These same questions could be used to guide group discussions for professional development of a school faculty.

School leaders who give positive answers to these questions already have beliefs aligned with the ISLLC and ELCC standards and the literature on parental and community relationships. The school leader must continue to review professional literature on this topic and attend in-service opportunities in order to develop strategies and mechanisms for establishing effective relationships with stakeholders outside the building.

After assessing your own beliefs regarding family and community collaboration, appraise the school community and the perceptions that parents and others have of the school. Face-to-face encounters provide the best basis for understanding these perceptions and are most influential in molding public opinion; the best way to do this is to get out into the community, shake hands, and go door to door. The greatest opportunity to influence and persuade and to hear and feel the community pulse occurs in more intimate settings than at the building level (Ubben, Hughes, and Norris 2001). Community and parental surveys may also be effective in obtaining the opinions and attitudes of external stakeholders. (Be sure to obtain professional guidance when designing any survey.) Additionally, use telephone and door-to-door interviews as a means for evaluating community views about the school. The goal is to get a random sampling of the population living in a particular school attendance area. The leader must be committed to getting periodic and regular information in order to tailor an effective school community relations plan (Ubben, Hughes, and Norris).

Assessment of the conditions and dynamics of the community will be the foundation for a school community relations plan. However, before actually devising a plan, there is a need to identify key communicators—influential people who are to be contacted when there is a need to disseminate or gather information quickly about the school. These people will usually have an identified interest in the school and are very significant because they interact with large numbers of people and are trusted. While key communicators will play many roles in the school, this group should play an even greater role in the creation and implementation of a school community relations plan (Ubben, Hughes, and Norris 2001).

How can school leaders identify these key communicators? A simple and easy to implementing strategy is to be a good listener. During any conversations, telephone discussions, or e-mails, be alert to names mentioned. Kaffeeklatsches like those described earlier in this chapter would also be a helpful source of identifying names. Begin to note these names in your computer, on index cards, or in a notebook, and keep tallies by each name as they are repeated in different contexts. Soon, a pattern of influential people (key communicators) in the community will begin to emerge.

The School Community Relations Plan

As briefly discussed, the authors believe that the goal of a school community relations plan is to find ways to involve many community members/groups and parents in the educational process as a way to help students to learn. An effective school–community plan is prepared in advance, organized, and ongoing. Communication and collaboration is the very premise of the process, and it should

Table 4.1

School Community Relations Plan

- Specifies the goals and objectives
- Identifies parents and specific community members and groups for partnerships
- Determines how communication and collaboration will be carried out
- Specifies when and how frequently communication should take place
- Identifies the person(s) who is/are responsible for each activity outlined in the plan

---

Source: Pawlas, G. 1995. *The Administrator's Guide to School Community Relations.* New York: Eye on Education.

be a two-way and reciprocal transaction. Ultimately, the school community relations program should build morale, goodwill, cooperation, and support. An effective school community relations plan should be a written plan that describes who says what to whom, through which channels, and with what effects (Pawlas 1995). Specific components of the written school community relations plan are identified in Table 4.1.

This plan should be based on solid action. The National School Public Relations Association (NSPRA 1999) stated that 90 percent of school public relations could be traced back to what is done in the school. Much can be accomplished if an effective school public relations plan is in place; however, the overall goal is to achieve the best possible education for the children who attend the school. Additionally, the plan should be written to include a multitude of techniques for communicating with parents and community members. It is important that educators establish and maintain public and parental confidence in the school in order to secure support. Once support and interest in the school are achieved, communication must be ongoing throughout the year.

Finally, a school relations plan must promote two-way communications. While it is important for the educators to share information about the school, it is equally important to be able to continuously gather opinions from the external stakeholders. The very premise of site-based management is a format of shared leadership and decision making. Parents and community members must be given a voice. The school leader can create a system of two-way communication in many ways. Having face-to-face interactions; conducting carefully designed surveys; facilitating meetings, forums, and discussion groups; and offering a telephone hotline for community members, online chat rooms, e-mail, blogs, and automatic mailing list servers are all ways to promote the sharing of ideas and opinions about the school.

Reaching Out to All Families

A review of the literature to date has shown unequivocally that involving parents in the education of their children results in increased student performance at all grade levels, regardless of educational background or social status. Effective family involvement opens the lines of communication between home and school and also supports parents who attempt to help their children in the educational process. School leaders must look beyond the traditional open house programs, PTA meetings, and annual parent–teacher conferences in order to achieve effective relationships with parents. Principals must implement various ways to communicate with parents such as newsletters, bulletin boards, the school marquee, informal notes, e-mail, and a school Web site. Parents should also be solicited to volunteer and aid in the school and in classrooms. School leaders must invite parents to be on committees and share in the decision making relevant to the school. When including parents on committees, the school leader must ensure that representation on the committee reflects the school and community demographics.

While educators may employ many strategies to involve parents in the educational process, an element of disconnection may still exist. School leaders must realize that the diversity and socioeconomic status of the community may hinder effective school and parental collaboration. Many families may still feel that their interests are not fully taken into account and may be reluctant to get involved. Again, the school principal must be willing and able to recognize the extent of this disconnection and make an extra effort to communicate and collaborate with these families. Adopt specific and appropriate mechanisms for making hard-to-reach families feel welcome at school. Table 4.2 provides some suggestions for including minority and economically disadvantaged parents in the educational process. The list is not all-inclusive; additional innovative strategies that meet the needs of the particular school community should be created.

Sadly, many parents, especially poorer families or recent immigrants or minorities, have been made to feel they are not welcome in the schools. Other parents may have memories that are unpleasant from the days when they were students or from when their older children were in school. Thus, they will not be comfortable coming to school functions, even conferences, or seeking assistance for their child. Or, if they do attend, they may have a preset notion that the experience will be negative and that the "school" cannot be trusted. Effective school leaders go to those families who, for any reason, will not come to them. We suggest setting aside at least one half day a week to visit the communities within the larger community where families who may not traditionally be active in the school live. Knock on doors; introduce yourself; start by saying there is no problem, you are simply visiting to see what the school can do to make the student's experiences the most positive they can be. You will find it pleasant and enlightening to realize how grateful these families become for the interest shown by the school. The time spent doing this will pay you untold dividends in the future.

Table 4.2

Strategies for Communicating with Underrepresented Parents

- Communicate with the home in the home language.
- Help families to become more proficient in English.
- Help school staff to become more proficient in languages other than English.
- Involve faculty/staff in interpreting language for others in the school.
- Recognize that households do not necessarily consist of the traditional nuclear family; communication may not be with a parent.
- Use every opportunity to communicate signs of progress, exceptional effort, good behavior, and attendance.
- Make initial contacts with parents positive.
- Ensure that students are not penalized for having limited financial resources.
- Do not stereotype or assume you know how a particular child will think or behave based on his or her ethnic background.
- Provide in-service to teachers and other administrators to learn more about the cultures represented in the school.
- Extend school or office hours to accommodate parents' work schedules.
- Arrange contacts in neutral settings or do home visits.
- Organize regular principal interaction sessions with 10 to 12 parents at a time.

Source: Barbour, C., N. H. Barbour, and P. A . Scully 2005. *Families, Schools, and Communities: Building Partnerships for Educating Children.* 3rd ed. Upper Saddle River, NJ: Prentice Hall.

Additionally, it is critical to have these disenfranchised families become part of the decision-making bodies in the school. School leaders should actively seek minority parents to serve on the PTA board, the school site-based management committee, and other real or quasi governance groups in the school. We recommend that at least one faculty meeting, one PTA executive committee meeting, one site-based management team meeting, and one general PTA meeting be conducted in a setting in an underrepresented community each semester.

The most important factor for overcoming barriers with families is the commitment and active involvement of the school leader. As the ISLLC and ELCC standards indicate, an effective school leader should be dedicated to building strong partnerships with families and communities in order to promote the success of all children. School leaders across the nation are building strong partnerships with great success. One such example is Boston's David A. Ellis School, where administrators, teachers, and parents are cooperating with the Institute for Responsive Education to make families equal participants in their children's education. This school has established a clothing exchange, classes for adult education, parent workshops, and breakfast meetings to draw parents into the school on a regular basis (Barclay and Boone 1995).

Additionally, Hawthorne Year-Round Elementary School in California created an accountability program in which parents and teachers are brought together to review standardized reading test data. Parents are contacted by telephone and mail; family homework projects are instituted that encourage reading at home; and a series of family seminars are conducted on such topics as homework help, discipline, and reading. Parents feel free to visit the classroom teachers and administrators before, during, and after school (Cohn-Vargas and Grose 1998).

Another strong model for parental involvement is the Comer School Development Process, established over 35 years ago by James Comer and Yale University. Comer created a governance and management team that includes parents, teachers, and support personnel. This model utilizes six developmental pathways to characterize the line along which children mature—physically, cognitively, psychologically, language facility, socially, and ethically. The parents and teachers use the six developmental pathways as a framework for making decisions that will benefit children. In schools using the Comer Process, far more is expected from the students than just cognitive development (Barbour, Barbour, and Scully 2005). Payne and Diamond (2001) note that the Comer Process includes several strategies that are implemented in school reform models today, including shared decision making, greater parent and community involvement, collaboration within and outside of the school, and specific services for individual students. These researchers go on to say that to do the above will require school leaders whose style includes collaboration, not placing blame, and willingness to share their power.

All of the above programs have resulted in gains in standardized test scores, grades, attendance, and student perseverance as well as a decrease in disciplinary referrals. Many established programs and models can be implemented. School leaders can create an eclectic school plan that meets the needs of a particular school community by drawing on components from a variety of successful models.

Involving the Broader Community

Just as the composition and makeup of families vary, so does the configuration of the community. Educators must also find ways to link the community to the school to promote student success. School leaders must not overlook the resources and opportunities that the community can bring to the educational process. Most communities have service agencies, political establishments, businesses or a business round-table whose focus is on education, a ministerial coalition, service and civic clubs, and other social cultural organizations that can provide children with the knowledge, values, and social skills needed to be successful. Some of the community organizations will make a deliberate effort to reach out to students and their families, while others may not be sure of ways in which they can help schools. The school leader must be able to connect the school and the community and solicit support in new and innovative ways.

Effective leaders in many schools have established successful collaborative ventures that have improved the education of students. In some schools, educators work with a single agency, while others collaborate with an alliance of several organizations. Schools in Texas and Tennessee have had success with the Adopt-a-School program. Through this program, coordinators identify needs of the schools and resources of businesses and then try to match schools to the appropriate businesses, tutors, pen pals, and mentors. Business-sponsored scholarships are awarded to teachers and students, and fund-raising events are held to benefit the school (Barbour and Barbour 1997).

The Alliance Schools is another thriving model that school leaders are using to improve student achievement. In this model, businesses and organizations can provide a multitude of resources to the school. At Morningside Middle School in Texas, standardized test scores went up, funds were garnered for a new library, health services were established, and numerous after-school enrichment programs were created (Hatch 1998), all as a result of partnerships with businesses and other organizations external to the school. Again, a myriad of established programs offer ways for school leaders to promote community involvement, or you can tailor a program that fits the needs of your particular school. In any case, broad community involvement can contribute to increased student achievement by helping to improve:

- The physical conditions, resources, and constituencies that support learning.
- The attitudes and expectations of parents, teachers, and students.
- The depth and quality of the learning experiences in which parents, teachers, and students participate (Hatch 1998, p. 16).

The Role of the Internal Public

In order for new and continuing principals to be successful at establishing and maintaining strong external partnerships, they must concentrate much effort on improving the relationships with the faculty, staff, and students inside the building. Individuals who are involved in the school, work in the school, or have a direct responsibility for the school can be critical factors in establishing effective school–community relations. These people include the students, the professional staff, the support staff, the central office staff, and the board of education. Experienced leaders contend that the school's internal populace is a powerful public relations force because of the credibility that has been established in the community.

Community members and parents form opinions and perceptions of the school based on information received from employees of the school and school district, and students who attend the school. Each member of the school staff— teachers, office personnel, instructional aides, cafeteria aides, nurses, custodians, crossing guards, and bus drivers—contributes to the school's image. As a school leader, work to improve the attitudes, skills, relationships, and perceptions of the internal public will be needed in order to gain community and parental support. A school's own staff is key to good school community relations.

Several years ago, the National School Public Relations Association (1986) conducted a survey to ascertain the public's opinions on credibility inside the school. A majority of the respondents believed that the custodian is the most believable person in the school. The second most believable person, according to the survey, was the school bus driver, followed by the cooks, secretaries, teachers, and then the school principal. These key staff members have an important role to play in the endeavor to solicit parental and community support, and the school leader must strive to make these people feel positive about the school.

There are many ways to work with the school's internal public to gain support and interest from external stakeholders. Aim to recognize and acknowledge each and every school employee. Make an effort to include a variety of staff members in school activities and meetings. Invite head custodians, the cafeteria manager, and the office secretary to give updates at the school's faculty meetings. Provide opportunities for them to participate in open house and talk to parents at other school functions. Invite all staff members to school celebrations and other events that are relevant to the entire staff. Be sure support staff has voting representation on site-based management teams. Make the entire staff aware of school district issues that affect the school, such as changes in boundaries and changes in school clientele. The goal is to create a climate of engagement that reflects the importance of everyone and their ideas at the school. By improving staff morale, the likelihood that the external public will have a better perception of the school is greatly enhanced.

The school secretary plays a very influential role in school–community relations. Beginning principals and experienced leaders who are new to a school need to sit down with the school secretary and discuss how to handle telephone calls and greet visitors. It may be helpful for the school secretary to attend workshops such as diversity training, communication skills, and customer service. The school leader and secretary could collaboratively determine what training may be helpful. An effective school secretary needs a ready smile, a kind voice, and an understanding and willingness to be of help to parents and community members who come to the school. These skills may be even more important than technical and office skills, for the school secretary is the person at the school who answers the most questions and talks to more parents than any other person (Barclay and Boone 1995).

One critical key to an effective school relations plan is effective classroom teachers. Good teaching not only helps students learn, but it also earns the respect, goodwill, and confidence of parents and other community members. The principal must help teachers understand that they make impressions when they talk and listen to students and parents, respond to questions, and respond to concerns and problems. Make it clear that there is an expectation for teachers to initiate and maintain communication with parents. Insist that they communicate with parents early and often about student progress, achievement, and discipline. Among the principal's most important responsibilities is to attract and retain quality teachers and improve the classroom skills that keep students actively engaged and learning.

Every encounter with a parent or community member presents an opportunity to build support for the school. To help school staff and teachers appreciate their specific responsibilities for involving parents and community members in the educational process, establish specific goals that advance strong school–community partnerships. Clearly convey expectations that all staff and faculty will implement strategies such as these:

- Speak favorably of the school in the community.
- Discuss and explain what is happening in the school in a positive way.
- Be friendly and courteous to school visitors and substitute teachers.
- Be a good citizen; take part in community service projects and organizations.
- Stay informed about what is happening in your school and school district. Know the facts before discussing events and plans.
- If you hear a rumor or criticism, don't let it grow or spread. Share it with the principal so that the correct information can be communicated.
- Be a model of positive attitude and hard work so that the students will have the correct model to follow and talk about outside the school (Pawlas 1995, p. 4).

The students, inarguably a key communication link, are perhaps the school's most important public relations factor. Not only are they the parents' main source of information about school; the way they feel about their school and the way they speak about their experiences goes directly to the community at large. A strong curriculum and good teachers constitute the backbone of a positive school image. Students also need to feel cared for and respected. The new or continuing principal can do much to create a positive environment for students. Know them by name. Recognize them for achievement, progress, good behavior—even birthdays. Publicize their accomplishments. Maintain and use student advisory groups. Whenever it makes sense to do so, involve them in school decision-making processes.

In conclusion, the school's internal public plays an important part in establishing and maintaining relationships with the parents and the community.

While it is important for school administrators to involve external stakeholders in the educational process, there must be a concentrated focus on the internal populace of the school. School leaders must create a positive, inviting, and warm school culture for students, staff, and teachers. Those individuals with direct ties to the school have much credibility in the community and can be a determining factor in the success of school–community relations.

More Research Needed

More research is needed on different forms and functions of community involvement. This research would help educators and scholars better understand and integrate community connections into a comprehensive program that encourages student learning and success (Sanders 2001). School leaders must continue to regularly survey their communities and parents in order to create a school plan that meets the needs of everyone involved. School principals should build on successful strategies but continue to devise strategies that expand on the initial successes. Additionally, school leaders must evaluate the success of their own school program to learn which efforts are most productive and to improve those that are not.

We encourage new and continuing principals to maintain ties with university or college educational leadership programs. In Table 4.3, we offer a model staff development plan that links professional development with school improvement. The example given here specifies the Comer Process, but educational leadership programs offer rich resources for other paths to developing an effective school community relations plan as well. Professors can also lend expertise in designing community and/or staff satisfaction surveys.

Table 4.3

Building a School Community Relations Program: A Model Staff Development Plan for New Principals	
Staff Development Activities	**Assessment/Demonstration of Knowledge**
School district will work in conjunction with the university. Educational researcher will work with new principals to design, implement, and analyze a survey for ascertaining how parents and community members perceive the school.	New principals will use the data gleaned from the survey to begin planning for school year. New principals will use the information to determine changes and improvement in the school.

Table 4.3

Building a School Community Relations Program *(continued)*	
Staff Development Activities	**Assessment/Demonstration of Knowledge**
School district will invite a representative from the National Network of Partnerships to give in-service, providing background information on school, family, and community partnerships and engage attendees in applying the ideas and approaches in their own schools. New principals will learn about the School Action Team's role in community involvement and begin drafting a school community relations plan.	New principals will present information learned to staff. School leader will develop an action team in the school. Action Team and the principal will write and implement a school community relations plan.
New principals will attend a district-sponsored symposium on education and equity. The symposium will include other educators, nonprofit organization leaders, and other prominent community members. The discussion will focus on the changing demographic nature of the district and the implications for standardized test scores. The discussion will also highlight how school partnerships with parents and community can assist students in reaching accountability goals.	In conjunction with the school Action Team, new principals will devise a list of strategies that will increase involvement of immigrant families in the school. New principal will do home visits and install a school telephone hotline that gives information in English and Spanish.
New principals will receive in-service from a representative of the Comer Regional Development Center. Presenter will disseminate information and explain the process of becoming a Comer school. New principal will visit schools that have successfully implemented the Comer model.	New principals will critique the schools they visited in a written report to the superintendent and include a recommendation for a school district adoption of the Comer model.

The Challenge

The increasingly diverse nature of society, communities, and schools presents certain challenges that can serve to inhibit communication and collaboration between schools and external stakeholders. Not only is our society characterized by varying family configurations, economic backgrounds, and racial and ethnic groups; there are a multitude of differing lifestyles, beliefs, and values in our social milieu. The school leader must view this diversity as beneficial to the school and give credence to individuals and groups with values and expectations that may conflict with the traditional norms of educators in the school and community.

School–community relations will serve to enhance the opportunities and advance learning for children. School leaders must understand the dynamics of the community and work to communicate and collaborate with parents and community members with cooperation and mutuality. In an effort to establish and maintain successful relationships, school leaders must create and implement strategies and an ongoing, comprehensive school community relations plan. As it is indicated in ISLLC Standard 4, the school principal must be able to stimulate a vested interest and a shared responsibility for student learning.

It is of vital importance for the principal to intertwine an educational public relations committee as part of the planning to attain the school vision. Members of this group will be entrusted with planning and subsequent systematic monitoring to help improve the school-community relations programs and services in their schools. The focus should be to stimulate a comprehensive two-way communications process that combines internal and external publics, with the main goal of stimulating better understanding of the roles, objectives, accomplishments, and needs of the school. This committee will oversee and be able to interpret public attitudes, identify and help shape recommendations for policies and procedures in the public interest, and carry on involvement and information activities that earn public understanding and support.

Suggested Readings

Fiore. D. 2006. *School Community Relations,* Second edition. Larchmont, NY: Eye On Education.

Pawlas, G. 2005. *The Administrator's Guide to School-Community Relations.* Larchmont, NY: Eye On Education.

Gallagher, D. Bagin and E. Moore. 2005. *The School and Community Relations,* Eighth Edition. Needham Heights, MA: Allyn and Bacon.

Suggested Activities

1. Complete a brief reflection about the material in Standard 4 in your reflection journal.

2. Conduct a trial kaffeeklatsch with six to eight participants. Prepare a written description of the process, including planning steps for the kaffeeklatsch, a summary of the discussion, and needed follow-up. Present the report for discussion by the whole class.

3. Locate a real school community relations plan and analyze it in writing based on the material found in Chapter 4.

4. Conduct a class discussion around the questions found under the heading "Assessing Perceptions." Format may be small groups, whole class, a combination of both, debate, an online forum, or another format.

MAJOR CHAPTER ASSIGNMENT

Using the case study *The Patriot,* written by Dr. Stanley A. Schainker, participate in a whole-class discussion to list the major issues, stated and unstated, in the case. Then, in small groups, develop strategies from the material found in Chapter 4 to address the stated as well as unstated issues.

The Patriot

by
Stanley A. Schainker, University of North Carolina at
Chapel Hill (with permission)

Jim Douglas, principal of Brown Creek Elementary School, shook his head in amazement. As he reflected on his five years as a high school social studies teacher, his course work and internship associated with his Masters in School Administration degree, his four years as a middle school assistant principal, his three years as a middle school principal, and now his two years as principal at Brown Creek, he could find nothing that prepared him to deal with the situation in which he currently found himself.

Mr. Douglas had always considered himself to be a strong patriot. Three close family members had served in the military. He displays the American flag from his front porch every day. The Fourth of July is a major celebration in his home. But now some parents, students, and teachers accuse him of being "un-American."

The problem started about two weeks ago, shortly after a terrorist attack on civilians in the United States. A group of about 20 parents came to him to demand that the school do more to promote patriotism. In particular, they wanted the Pledge of Allegiance recited by all students at the beginning of each day. They argued that students were frightened about the terrorists and needed to do something to fight back. They believed that reciting the Pledge each day would meet the students' needs.

Jim responded, "By compelling everyone to say the pledge, we would be trampling on the very freedoms we are trying to promote." He went on to say the staff had to be very sensitive to whether saying the Pledge might be offensive to some families in this very diverse community. In addition, while admitting that this might not be his decision to make alone, he would fight to protect the rights of the few even if it went against the wishes of the many. The district's policy on this issue was that it is a matter to be resolved by the school's site-based management team.

The 20 parents left Douglas's office very upset. They immediately launched a petition drive calling for the Pledge to be recited daily in the school. After three days, 70 percent of the school's parents had signed the petition. These parents also started a telephone campaign aimed at the superintendent and school board. Each of the board members and the Superintendent were receiving an average of 20 calls a day urging them to intervene to support patriotism and American values. Douglas also received calls from the commanders of the local American Legion and Veteran of Foreign Wars posts, who also noted American flags were not displayed in the classrooms. To compound the issue, for the last five days, parents and students had been gathering around the flagpole in front of the school before school started and reciting the Pledge. Even several teachers and other school staff had joined the now almost 200 participants. The local television news loved it and began featuring this story nightly. Editorials in the two local newspapers as well as letters to the editor were showing overwhelming support for requiring daily recitation of the Pledge in the school.

INDIVIDUAL OR CLASS REFLECTION

Examine educational documents on the topic of conflict and discuss some of the content from this chapter in relationship to the intention of this standard for principals.

Review Session for Chapters 1–4

Before you start on Chapter 5, this will be a good time to spend a few sessions reviewing some of the content from specific activities in Chapters 1–4.

ISLLC Standards Activity

Debate has swirled in recent years about whether principals demonstrate excellence, or even competence, in their chosen profession. Since school leaders have tremendous influence over students and learning, they must be knowledgeable about methods and strategies that better students' learning. When school leaders make decisions concerning students' learning, they must be guided by standards that promote success for all children. The ISLLC Standards ensure that principals are competent professionals who base their decisions on enhancing students' learning.

Why the ISLLC Standards Are Necessary

The ISLLC Standards:

◆ Ensure that principals demonstrate knowledge, inclinations, and performances that focus on teaching and learning.

◆ Facilitate the development of leadership skills that benefit both teachers and students.

◆ Insist that school leaders work collaboratively with parents, businesses, communities, and political leaders to facilitate students' learning.

◆ Promote the value of generating a positive school climate where all stakeholders can work to their maximum potential.

- Guarantee that the diverse groups of students entering schools are treated fairly and in an ethical manner.
- Encourage collaboration between states on topics such as reciprocity of licensure and principals' assessment.

Knowledge, Dispositions, and Performances

Each of the six ISLLC Standards is divided into three sections: knowledge, dispositions, and performances. The knowledge section ensures that a principal has understanding of theories, concepts, and strategies relevant to the standard. The dispositions segment advances the idea that the principal must transfer theories, concepts, and strategies to students and staff. The performance section encourages school administrators to engage in activities that promote successful completion of the relevant standard.

ISLLC Standard 1

A school administrator is an educational leader who promotes the success of all students by facilitating the development, articulation, implementation, and stewardship of a vision of learning that is shared and supported by the school community.

Scenario 1

Mrs. Johnson is the principal of a middle school located in an urban setting. The school has students from many diverse cultural backgrounds. The principal is currently reviewing the school's scores from the seventh-grade writing test. The scores improved from the previous year; however, they still fall short of her goals. The principal is determined to raise the writing scores but unsure of how to go about it. She decides to use ISLLC Standard 1 to better the scores.

Response

At the first meeting of the next school year, Mrs. Johnson asks her staff what improvements are necessary for the upcoming year. Several suggestions are made, and one includes bettering the writing scores. The school leader then informs her staff that her number one priority is to increase the writing test scores. Next, she solicits feedback about why improving student writing is imperative. Mrs. Johnson emphasizes the belief that all schools should be learning communities focused on high standards of learning.

Before school begins, the school improvement team determines that more emphasis should be placed on writing. The team asks the language arts department for any suggestions or ideas to better students' writing. The department decides to incorporate a mandatory writing block into all language classes. The principal agrees and implements the suggestion. Also, throughout the school year, the principal recognizes staff members who better students writing.

Was the response reasonable? Why or why not?

Explanation

Mrs. Johnson and her staff have utilized knowledge, dispositions, and performances from ISLLC Standard 1 to improve their seventh-grade writing scores. The school used effective communication and consensus building to develop a school vision of high standards of learning. The staff also implemented educational programs based on their vision. In addition, ceremonies and praise recognized successful completion of the vision. Green (2001) says that to help children reach performance standards, a vision must be shared by school members. The response to Scenario 1 demonstrates a vision of learning supported by the school community.

Do you agree? Why or why not?

ISLLC Standard 2

A school administrator is an educational leader who promotes the success of all students by advocating, nurturing, and sustaining a school culture and instructional program conducive to student learning and staff professional growth.

Scenario 2

Mr. Stewart is the principal of a large suburban high school. The school has above-average test scores on state-mandated tests. During the course of every school day, the principal does numerous classroom informal observations. In the course of the snapshots, the school administrator notices that most teachers are utilizing the lecture method. The school leader is concerned that many students are not learning to their full potential. The principal decides to employ ISLLC Standard 2 to better teachers' instructional presentation.

Response

The school administrator calls a staff meeting where he praises all teachers for their hard work and dedication to students' learning. Next, he informs the staff that next week, university professors will come and teach the staff a variety of instructional styles. Mr. Stewart emphasizes that the professional development will make staff lifelong learners dedicated to bettering pupils' learning. During the course of the year, the principal honors any teacher utilizing an instructional strategy taught by the professors. He also decides to compare the state-mandated test scores of students whose teachers largely lectured with those of students whose teachers integrated the new instructional strategies into their classroom instruction.

Was the response reasonable? Why or why not?

Explanation

Mr. Stewart has made use of knowledge, dispositions, and performances from ISLLC Standard 2 to sustain an instructional program conducive to student learning and staff professional growth. He used professional development as a way to make staff lifelong learners and understand principles of effective instruction. The principal also praised staff, making them feel valued and important. In addition, comparing students' test scores, based on the instructional strategy of the teacher, will allow the principal to analyze data on methods used to better the school's instructional program. Green (2001) says, "it is the principal's responsibility to have adequate and appropriate staff in the building" (p. 26). The response to Scenario 2 shows how a school culture can be fostered to promote students' learning.

Do you agree? Why or why not?

ISLLC Standard 3

A school administrator is an educational leader who promotes the success of all students by ensuring management of the organization, operations, and resources for a safe, efficient, and effective learning environment.

Scenario 3

Mrs. Thomas is the principal at Lincoln High School. For the past few years, the school has received a grant that allowed it to purchase over $50,000 worth of science equipment. However, during the course of informal and formal observations, Mrs. Thomas notices that only a small portion of the equipment is being used. The chair of the science department informs her that the materials are spread throughout teachers' classrooms as well as lost in the school. The principal decides to use ISLLC Standard 3 to ensure efficient management of the school's resources.

Response

Meeting with the science team, the principal asks them to locate resources and materials, then use Microsoft Excel to complete an inventory of science equipment and resources. She also designates one room as the "library" for all science materials and institutes a sign-out system for teachers wishing to use them. During the inventory, the principal encourages feedback and asks science teachers to brainstorm any methods of improving the process.

Was the response reasonable? Why or why not?

Explanation

The school administrator has utilized knowledge, dispositions, and performances from ISLLC Standard 3 to ensure efficient management of school resources. The school used current technology and issues relating to use of space to enhance learning and teaching. The science teachers, with help from the principal, accepted responsibility and confronted and resolved the problem in a timely, decisive manner. The new system maximized opportunities for students' learning. The response to Scenario 3 shows how a principal can efficiently manage a school so that maximum student learning will take place.

Do you agree? Why or why not?

ISLLC Standard 4

A school administrator is an educational leader who promotes the success of all students by collaborating with families and community members, responding to diverse community interests and needs, and mobilizing community resources.

Scenario 4

Mr. Washington is the principal at Harriet Tubman Elementary School. The school serves a diverse group of students, many from low-income, single-parent households. The school has below-average test scores on state-mandated tests and also has many discipline problems. The principal realizes that the school needs help, so he turns to the families of the students and the local community for support. He will attempt to collaborate with families and the community to better students' learning and behavior.

Response

Mr. Washington decides to send a letter home to all parents, explaining some of the school's problems. In the letter, he invites volunteers who wish to serve as tutors, mentors, and buddies to send back a simple form indicating their willingness to help the school. The principal also makes an appointment with representatives of a local corporation to solicit similar volunteers. The principal entrusts the school improvement team with the responsibility of training the volunteers and coordinating the scheduling. During the course of the year, Mr. Washington sends the families and the business partner feedback, informing them of program results and inviting suggestions for improving the process.

Was the response reasonable? Why or why not?

Explanation

The principal has utilized knowledge, dispositions, and performances from ISLLC Standard 4 to better the school. The school leader, by communicating with and using community resources, has made an effort to increase students' learning. By establishing partnerships with families and an area business, the school has taken steps toward building a community. Thomson (1992) believes "school leaders who use the broad human and material resources of their communities creatively will provide lively educational experiences for their pupils" (p. 12). The response to Scenario 4 demonstrates how a principal can effectively communicate with the community to create a successful learning environment for children.

Do you agree? Why or why not?

ELCC Standards Activity

ELCC Standard 1 (Standard 1.0)
Candidates who complete the program are educational leaders who have the knowledge and ability to promote the success of all students by facilitating the development, articulation, implementation, and stewardship of a school or district vision of learning supported by the school community.

Why ELCC Standard 1 Is Necessary

The first step in changing any school for the better is advancing a vision. McCall (1994) says it is a vision that starts meaningful, creative, and enriching change. Greenfield (1987) believes a principal must form a realistic vision and be able to effectively communicate it in such a way that the school community carries it out. Standard 1 is necessary because it makes future or current principals focus on students' learning, on developing a collegial school climate, and on promoting a schoolwide commitment to children.

Do you agree? Why or why not?

ELCC Standard 2 (Standard 2.0)

Candidates who complete the program are educational leaders who have the knowledge and ability to promote the success of all students by promoting a positive school culture, providing an effective instructional program, applying best practice to student learning, and designing comprehensive professional growth plans for staff.

Why ELCC Standard 2 Is Necessary

Well-defined courses and staff development seminars can offer graduate students and beginning principals many opportunities to learn curriculum and instructional leadership skills to guide a faculty to provide children with an effective instructional program. Since children learn through a variety of learning styles, principals must understand a variety of teaching models. Course requirements should demand that prospective principals demonstrate knowledge of differing instructional designs and models by teaching.

Principals stand at the crossroads of teaching and learning. Joyce, Weil, and Calhoun (2000) state that "as students master information and skills, the result of each learning experience is not only the control they learn, but the increased ability they acquire to approach future learning tasks and to create programs of study for themselves" (p. 10). If children are to become problem solvers, critical thinkers, effective decision makers, and productive members of our democratic society, excellent teachers who utilize best teaching practices must teach them. Principals must provide instructional leadership so teachers can teach and children can learn.

Do you agree? Why or why not?

ELCC Standard 3 (Standard 3.0)

Candidates who complete the program are educational leaders who have the knowledge and ability to promote the success of all students by managing the organization, operations, and resources in a way that promotes a safe, efficient, and effective learning environment.

Why ELCC Standard 3 Is Necessary

The resources allocated to schools are never enough. Teachers are too often underpaid, facilities are typically too old, and technology used generally lags behind that used in other professions. With all of these obstacles, one of the most important parts of schooling is to create a safe, supportive learning environment for children. Thomson (1992) says, "In an efficiently run organization, in which immediate problems are handled in a decisive and timely way, responsibilities are clearly delineated and delegated, and the protection of the time and safety of students and staff is a high priority" (p. 20). When schools run smoothly with resources and operations at maximum efficiency, students have an opportunity to learn.

Do you agree? Why or why not?

ELCC Standard 4 (Standard 4.0)

Candidates who complete the program are educational leaders who have the knowledge and ability to promote the success of all students by collaborating with families and other community members, responding to diverse community interests and needs, and mobilizing community resources.

Why ELCC Standard 4 Is Necessary

Schools are a microcosm of society. The values and beliefs of society are taught in schools. Therefore, community members are concerned about whether schools are producing children who embody these values and can function in our democratic society. Parents have the right and obligation to know whether their children are learning how to become productive adults. The community, with resources and knowledge, has the ability to facilitate student growth. Ubben, Hughes, and Norris (2001) say community members must be informed and involved in school happenings. They argue, "If school principals do not use available means to interact with members of the community, the school will become static and unresponsive to changing community and societal needs" (p. 343). If schools effectively interact with communities, there will be many adults helping the school learning community.

Do you agree? Why or why Not?

We hope that these activities have given you a good review and perhaps an even better working understanding of their intentions in actual school situations. You are ready to begin Chapter 5. We will have Review II at the end of Chapter 7.

5

Standard Five:
Integrity, Fairness, and
Ethics as an Essential of
Leadership Development

A leader's role is to raise people's aspirations for what they can become and to release their energies so they will try to get there.
—David R. Gergen

ISLLC Standard 5	ELCC Standard 5
A school administrator is an educational leader who promotes the success of all students by acting with integrity, fairness, and in an ethical manner.	*Candidates who complete the program are educational leaders who have the knowledge and ability to promote the success of all students by acting with integrity, fairly, and in an ethical manner.*

In the role of the instructional leader, no standard is more important to the development of the entire school community than the principles of integrity, fairness, and ethical behavior. Imperative to the role of the principal is the ability and disposition to model high standards of personal and professional behavior. The principal's leadership in the areas of integrity, fairness, and ethical behavior creates a framework for high achievement for teachers, students, and staff. It is the principal who sets and models high standards for the entire school and insists that these are upheld.

After all, as Professor Patrick Duignan (2005) from New Zealand puts it so succinctly, "It is not budgeting, mission statements or strategic plans that keep school leaders awake at night, but issues to do with people, and these involve values and ethics. What is needed is better preparation of school leaders to develop all-round capable human beings who know themselves and their own values" (retrieved from www.e-lead.org, August 16, 2005). And the authors believe that school leaders and future leaders who have a high level of integrity, hold honesty as a universal value, and behave fairly in all actions regardless of personal and professional loss can be the model that teachers and students wish to emulate. While this standard focuses specifically on the actions of the principal, we believe that most of these values will be developed by the time a person enters the profession. In transforming the role of the principalship, we have decided to refocus much of this chapter on the role the principal can serve as model or guiding light not only from an administrative role, but from the role of helping to build or integrate curricula for students for the greatest outcomes associated with integrity, fairness, and honestly—values that have been compromised in the greater society and are often absent in the school, and even more so, in the instructional process to children. Whether formal or informal, this may become what Covey (2004) describes as the *8th Habit* and the business leaders throughout the world have taken from Goleman's work on emotional intelligence (the developer of *Emotional Intelligence*) to form emotional leadership. We support the work of Michael Fullan and others who focus on moral leadership and how it can serve as a catalyst for others. We believe the actions of educational leaders are watched closely by many stakeholders in the process of schooling. If role modeling has any true value; this is a wonderful place to start.

To summarize our point, the authors believe that the principal must always be aware of the influence of the principalship on the school and the community. That influence on teachers, students, and staff may be positive or negative. Therefore, integrity, fairness, and ethics must be at the forefront of every action taken by the principal.

In fact, in order to truly adhere to a deeper intent and what we see as the transformative purpose of ISLLC Standard 5, we recommend that school leaders act in conjunction with an established code of ethics. This could be a code established by a professional leadership association, a code collaboratively developed among peers, a code developed with a faculty that reflects a collaboratively developed vision, or a code developed individually. Figures 5.1, 5.2, and 5.3

Figure 5.1

Statement of Ethics for School Administrators
NAESP Policy Statement 1100.3

An educational administrator's professional behavior must conform to an ethical code. The code must be idealistic and at the same time practical, so that it can apply reasonably to all educational administrators. The administrator acknowledges that the schools belong to the public they serve for the purpose of providing educational opportunities to all. However, the administrator assumes responsibility for providing professional leadership in the school and community. This responsibility requires the administrator to maintain standards of exemplary professional conduct. It must be recognized that the administrator's actions will be viewed and appraised by the community, professional associates, and students. To these ends, the administrator subscribes to the following statements of standards:

1. Makes the well-being of students the fundamental value in all decision making and actions.
2. Fulfills professional responsibilities with honesty and integrity.
3. Supports the principle of due process and protects the civil and human rights of all individuals.
4. Obeys local, state, and national laws.
5. Implements the governing board of education's policies and administrative rules and regulations.
6. Pursues appropriate measures to correct those laws, policies, and regulations that are not consistent with sound educational goals.
7. Avoids using positions for personal gain through political, social, religious, economic, or other influence.
8. Accepts academic degrees or professional certification only from duly accredited institutions.
9. Maintains the standards and seeks to improve the effectiveness of the profession through research and continuing professional development.
10. Honors all contracts until fulfillment or release.

illustrate codes of ethics developed by leadership associations. Perhaps in the future, individual schools, classrooms, and even individual students (based on developmental levels) can develop personal codes including the elements of fairness, honesty, and integrity and always act with the highest ethical behavior.

The principal's actions and dispositions create an atmosphere that is in keeping with an ideal learning environment. Principals who begin with the end in

Figure 5.2

Association for Supervision and Curriculum Development (ASCD)
Code of Ethics

- ASCD's mission can only be realized through a common code of ethics upheld by our officers, board of directors, and staff.
- We expect integrity, honesty, and trustworthiness in our work; courage in our decisions; and dedication to ASCD's values and beliefs.
- We expect responsible action on behalf of the organization and are accountable and transparent to our constituents and to one another. We share information when appropriate without sacrificing confidentiality.
- We expect to be treated and to treat others with respect. We respect the opinions of and the differences among individuals.
- We expect fairness to be evident in our actions internally and externally. We are equitable in our decisions and mindful of their impact on other groups and people.
- We expect our actions to demonstrate our care for others and the community as a whole. We support each other in a humane manner. We care about the well-being of each other, the community, and the Association.

mind understand what is really important to them as they set out to lead a school. The milieu in which the leader operates should, above all, include integrity, fairness, and ethical behavior.

Historically, schools were the institutions that helped to teach and nurture high moral values in students (Lickona 1993). All educators were expected to be of the highest moral character. The principal and the teacher were held in the highest esteem and valued, if not imitated. Society believed one of the roles of the school was to mold the child into a better person, and schools accepted the role and acted accordingly.

Over the years, society's values changed to uplift the person as having individual rights, and the emphasis on responsibility to society diminished (Lickona 1993). However, there has been a recent return to the uplifting of universal moral values and the teaching of moral education (Huffman 1993). This is now in vogue as character education. Many educators and other citizens applaud the resurgence of an emphasis on educating the whole student as opposed to teaching mere academics in isolation from moral values.

Figure 5.3

American Association of School Administrators (AASA)
Statement of Ethics for School Administrators

An educational administrator's professional behavior must conform to an ethical code. The code must be idealistic and at the same time practical so that it can apply reasonably to all educational administrators.

The administrator acknowledges that the schools belong to the public he or she serves for the purpose of providing educational opportunities to all. However, the administrator assumes responsibility for providing professional leadership in the school and community. The responsibility requires the administrator to maintain standards of exemplary professional conduct. It must be recognized that the administrator's actions will be viewed and appraised by the community, professional associates and students.

To these ends, the administrator subscribes to the following statements of standards.

The educational administrator:

1. Makes the well-being of students the fundamental value of all decision making and actions.

2. Fulfills professional responsibilities with honesty and integrity.

3. Supports the principle of due process and protects the civil and human rights of all individuals.

4. Obeys local, state, and national laws and does not knowingly join or support organizations that advocate, directly or indirectly, the overthrow of the government.

5. Implements the governing board of education's policies, and administrative rules and regulations.

6. Pursues appropriate measures to correct those laws, policies, and regulations that are not consistent with sound educational goals.

7. Avoids using positions for personal gain through political, social, religious, economic or other influences.

8. Accepts academic degrees or professional certification only from duly accredited institutions.

9. Maintains the standards and seeks to improve the effectiveness of the profession through research and continuing professional development.

10. Honors all contracts until fulfillment, release or dissolution mutually agreed upon by all parties to contract.

—Adopted by AASA Executive Committee, 1981

Source: Retrieved May 31, 2006, from www.aasa.org/about/content.cfm?ItemNumber=2157

Historical Perspectives

Historically, the major purposes of education served the development of smart people and good people simultaneously. The basic premises of American society were grounded in the belief that schools were to educate students to develop into moral, functioning members of society.

John Dewey, one of the most influential and effective educators of the 20th century, stressed the importance of teaching character education (Collinson 2001). In the past, moral education was an integral aspect of the education of the young child, and values were stressed in the schools on a daily basis. Good moral education was believed to be essential if young people were to grow up and become contributing members of society.

It was in the 1960s that society began to pull away from the traditional moral teachings in schools and to emphasize the importance and the rights of the individual (Lickona 1993). A survey of what made up the areas for concern in the public schools in the 1940s indicated that educators were concerned about "talking, chewing gum, making noise, running in the halls, getting out of turn in line, wearing improper clothing, and not putting paper in the wastebasket" (Huffman 1993). After 20 years of an emphasis on individual rights as opposed to societal concerns, the list in 1980 consisted of "drug abuse, alcohol abuse, pregnancy, suicide, rape, robbery, and assault" (Huffman). Clearly, areas of concern have become more serious, and educators have seen the need to do something to make schools safer so learning and teaching can occur in a comfortable environment.

Even more urgently, many people in the United States today are concerned about youth and crime in our society. According to Gutierrez, "expenditures concerning crime are at an all time high." Many citizens in the American society believe today's youth must be taught a sense of duty in the schools if they are not going to be taught values accepted by the community at home (Gutierrez 2001).

The Need for Moral Education in Schools

The teaching of certain standards by which one lives one's life has become important to many educators. The instructional leader must provide for the moral and ethical education of the students who attend the school. This is a practice from which all students can benefit, but it is especially important for those students who do not receive this instruction at home. In the United States, some students do not come to school with experiences that provide them with the structure and guidance to function well in society. The principal, working with the community, must ensure that this instruction in moral and ethical behavior is incorporated into the school instruction and that all members of the school community model it.

Chase (1998) says that all children need guidance and direction from caring adults. He contends that public school employees have a great influence on the lives of students. Indeed, the only adults who are more important to the child are that child's family and religious community (Chase 1998). Therefore, it is imperative that public school employees not only teach good morals and values, but live them as well. This becomes even more important for the child who comes from a home that cannot provide the value system that the child needs to learn to live in our society. In this way, schools must help children from these homes become responsible students who feel that adults do care about them. They must be taught how to stay focused, control their anger, and grow up to become functioning and mentally healthy adults (Lickona 1993).

Since the 1990s, educators have developed an initiative to restore good moral and ethical guidance to the public school system. Many character education programs are being implemented in the nation's schools in order to provide a formal framework for teaching good values. In addition, an emphasis on making good choices has been emphasized in the school culture in more informal ways. Restoring good moral education in the schools is a practice that society wants to see happening. It is an important responsibility of the principal to see that society is served in this respect.

Formal Character Education Programs

Currently, several different formal character education programs are being implemented in public schools. Among them are the Aspen Declaration on Character Education, the Character Education Partnership, and others that were developed to teach character education in a direct and formal way. They have produced books to guide in teaching their programs and periodicals to reinforce their principles. The ideas proposed in these books and programs have become very popular.

It is obvious that the return to the formal teaching of morals and values in the schools is a direct result of how bad society is perceived to have become. Schools have been commissioned to teach students the elements of good character and how to implement it into their own lives. Chase insists that basic values must be instilled into children: honesty, taking responsibility for one's actions, and having respect for others. He believes that these values are at the core of discipline and that learning cannot occur without them (Chase 1998). Formal character education in schools has its place when it is valued by the stakeholders in the school and when this is the preferred method of teaching good values. It is by no means the only way that good character can be developed in children.

Informal Character Education

Character education can be taught in a variety of more informal ways. The school community must model good choices, and the best examples of integrity, fairness, and ethics modeling must begin with the principal. It is the responsibility of the instructional leader to model an ideal standard and require its implementation in the school culture. Of course, to do so you must have already developed a good moral character and good values, chief among them integrity, fairness, and ethics. Covey states, "The essence of principle-centered living is making the commitment to listen to and live by conscience" (Covey 1994). As principal, you must let your conscience be the guide to implementing positive values in the school.

Integrity in Interactions with Staff

Since good moral character must be the focus of school interactions, all staff should be treated in a fair and ethical manner. **Trust** might be the most important word in a school leader's value set. Until trust is established with all stakeholder groups, there will be no real movement toward collaboration, a focus on student achievement, or implementation of a vision. The highest expectations for staff members must be a given, and the staff must be assured that the highest expectations extend to the school leader as well. The staff must know exactly what is expected and that those expectations are rooted in exemplary moral and ethical character. In addition, staff must be assured that you will treat all staff the same, with an emphasis on fairness and equity in actions toward teachers as well as custodians, cafeteria staff, and office staff. The principal must model integrity, fairness, and a strong sense of ethics if the school is to operate at the highest level. A sense of empathy toward all members of the school community is imperative.

How does a principal earn the trust of teachers? The following traits have been identified through research as especially effective in motivating teachers:

- Allow for discovery, exploration, variety and challenge.
- Provide high involvement with the task and high identity with the task, enabling work to be considered important and significant.
- Allow for active participation.
- Emphasize agreement with respect to broad purposes and values that bond people together at work.
- Permit outcomes within broad purposes to be determined by the worker.
- Encourage autonomy and self-determination. Allow persons to feel like "origins" of their own behavior rather than "pawns" manipulated from the outside.
- Encourage feelings of competence and control and enhance feelings of efficacy (Sergiovanni 1990, p. 129).

Thomas Sergiovanni (1992) refers to the heart, head, and hand of leadership. He says the heart is what the leader ". . . believes, values, dreams about, and is committed to. . . ." (7). The head, according to Sergiovanni, is the leader's practices developed through experience, and then the ability to reflect on these theories of practice and how they apply to specific situations. We describe the heart and the head. What about the hand? He goes on to say, "The head of leadership is shaped by the heart and drives the hand; in turn, reflections on decisions and actions affirm or reshape the heart and the head" (p. 7).

In another book, *Value-Added Leadership* (1990), Sergiovanni encourages leaders to develop followers as an alternative to leading through formal bureaucratic structures. He believes followers will be able to self-manage tasks, if allowed to be the leader. Again, it is the concept of trust. Neil Shipman, former director of ISLLC, has long espoused the principle that if a leader treats professionals as professionals, then these professionals will behave like professionals. This is not a complex concept. Teachers are quite capable of making their own decisions about instruction. If allowed to act as followers and not subordinates, they will commit to the collaboratively developed school vision.

Integrity in Interactions with Students

One principal wrote of setting the tone for character education in the school by teaching good values through class meetings and mentoring students. Pastor (2002) believes that we must prepare productive members of society, and we can do this only if we teach good character in our schools. This principal went further, even basing the school's discipline process on teaching good ethical principles. Respect, caring, and responsibility were the expected norms for all of the members of the school community in this school, and discipline did improve dramatically (Pastor 2002).

The entire school must be involved in the teaching of good moral education (Sizer and Sizer 1999). Words are good tools for teaching, but there is no substitute for modeling good ethical behavior. The true essence of a person is perceived in everything about that person, and there is no substitute for good moral character. It is difficult to pretend to be ethical and moral when daily actions attest to the opposite. It is imperative that good morals and good character pervade the school community.

Impact on School and Community

Values education is an intrinsic part of the teaching process and of the school community (Huffman 1993). Principals and teachers model and teach values by every word and action that they employ in and out of school. It is important, therefore, that principals and teachers be of high moral character. Part of the ISLLC Standard 5 states that a school administrator must respect the rights and dignity of everyone. If a principal does not treat a teacher, parent, or student with respect, that principal exhibits a lack of moral character. If a teacher does not treat a student with respect, that teacher violates an essential value (Huffman 1993). Teaching respect for others is possible only when respect for others is constantly modeled. Students will have little respect for teaching character education if they do not observe good character traits as part of the adult community. The model must come from the principal and pervade the school as a whole.

There is much emphasis today on schools achieving the highest goals possible. Striving for high achievement can create high stress on everyone in the school community, especially when the reputation of the school and the principal are under scrutiny. Scores on end-of-year standardized tests affect not only reputation but also monetary compensation in many districts.

Stress causes adverse reactions in some situations, and some members of the school community have allowed the stress of needing to increase achievement to cause actions that do not exemplify high moral character. In at least one school, a principal changed student answers on the end-of-grade tests to have the students score higher. When this was discovered, the principal was removed from the school, but the community knew what had occurred. This principal set an example of lack of moral character and good values that the community and, sadly, the students will remember.

Teachers and students feel the stress of high achievement as well. Everyone in the school community should have high expectations, but those expectations must be reasonable. If the standards are set impossibly high, the students and teachers will feel a sense of failure that does not foster a good learning environment. Teachers and students who feel powerless to achieve may just give up or resort to cheating. A teacher who allows cheating exhibits a lack of values to the students in the classroom (Huffman 1993). High expectations must be maintained in such a way that all members of the school community know that learning is important, but good moral values must prevail at all times.

Integrating Good Values

Vincent and Meche (2001) state that effective moral education is evident when students make good moral decisions based on what they have integrated into their lives, and these decisions must be consistent. Teachers are role models for students, and their teaching has a great impact on the lives of students and their behavior. It is important that teachers play an active role in the school community's effort to teach ethics and good problem solving. Whether teachers like it or not, students emulate their behavior and heed their words. It is essential that educators be moral and ethical people themselves. One of the most important roles of a principal is to hire moral and ethical teachers who care about nurturing children.

A caring school community is important. This is true whether it is an elementary, middle, or high school. In fact, a frequent complaint from high school students is that they are not known or cared about as people. It is important that members of the school community treat others well and that this caring carries over into society as a whole. Being empathetic can be taught, but empathy is a moral virtue that is best modeled. The model begins at the principal's door and should set the example for the school. An effective principal should genuinely care about students, teachers, and parents, and this should be apparent in every aspect of the principal's nature and actions.

The values of respect, responsibility, compassion, honesty, and civic participation are at the core (Hunter 2004). Students who hold these values naturally need to have the opportunity to implement them in their daily lives. Only within a nurturing environment can human beings attempt to act on moral rules and develop moral imagination (Fesmire 2001). It is precisely the school community that must be the environment for that nurturing. The belief that the schools must encourage good moral behavior has extended to public policy, and many legislatures have created laws that mandate the teaching of commonly held values (Hunter 2004).

The skills of civil behavior are important, and those skills can and must be taught. Sizer and Sizer (1999) describe them as "showing restraint, being willing to listen, having empathy, feeling responsible for something and some people beyond oneself and one's personal coterie of friends, being nice, and getting along in one's daily interactions." These skills are important in every phase of life, and the sooner they are integrated into one's basic character, the better. These skills are ones that will enable a more perfect society to be created in the future if they are properly implemented.

Respecting Diversity

School communities in the United States continue to see increasing diversity. As instructional leader of the school community, you guide its appreciation for that diversity. This means celebrating and embracing diversity in the school. Beginning in the elementary school and continuing into successive levels of the educational organization, integrity, fairness, and ethics must be taught to students of all cultures. According to Hunter (2000), psychologists believe that there are certain virtues that are innate in every person and in every culture, but these virtues and values must be taught and nurtured if they are to develop to their greatest potential. It is the school's responsibility to develop this potential, and it is the principal's responsibility to encourage it.

Modifying Instruction to Teach Values

Many opportunities for teaching integrity, fairness, and ethics exist in the curriculum already being used in the classroom (Myers 2001). Literature abounds with examples of what constitutes fairness, responsibility, truthfulness, and unselfishness, to name a few of the values that we want students to develop. Social studies, history, and current events can be used to teach right behavior from wrong. Students are exposed to moral dilemmas on television, in newspapers, on the Internet, and in magazines (Myers 2001). All of these media provide material for problem solving and discussing the moral issues and dilemmas that confront society today.

The physical education curriculum is rich with opportunities to teach character education to students as they interact with each other in games. In addition, the teacher conducting the activities provides a good role model for fairness, self-discipline, and conflict resolution. Crawford et al. (2001) believe that teaching ethics is positive role modeling and believes that good teachers are more likely to produce good students.

Lake states that even though moral environments may be evident in the classrooms with the rules, teacher attitudes, curriculum, and sports, these values need to be specifically taught and reinforced by adults in the school community. The daily interactions among students, staff, and administrators should teach and model good character every day. Students should have constant opportunity to examine what is good and put it into practice as they interact with others (Lake 2001).

Specific problems in the school community may be addressed with simple stories that the teacher makes up to address the problem. In this way, students can relate the problem in the story to problems in their own lives and discover the most appropriate ways of handling those problems (Myers 2001). Ethical problem solving is the key to reinforcing and integrating good moral character in children in their formative years. Good character can be developed, and good problem solvers will contribute to society in the future.

Caring and Morals

There is evidence that caring for students and teaching good moral values in schools has a positive effect that fans out and touches many lives. Donaldson (2001) writes to a former professor about teaching in a public high school that is a good example of diversity. The point of the letter is to tell the professor that he taught her a value that transcended one student in one classroom. It is an example of the power of caring and the impact that it can make on students' lives when a teacher models high expectations with that caring (Donaldson 2001). This is precisely the kind of modeling good character and good values that a principal of integrity must infuse into the school community.

The Moral Focused Principal (ELCC Standard 5)

Since the 1980s, researchers have placed the primary focus on changing roles in principal leadership. In the past 20 years, both the public and principals have demonstrated the major concern of the evolving role of the principalship. These changes have resulted from the increased demands of state and federal agencies, including the No Child Left Behind Act (NCLB). A 2004 survey of 925 principals working with grades kindergarten through 12 found that 88 percent of principals believe NCLB has enormously added to the principal's job responsibilities without consideration of needed resources ("Administrators weigh in," 2004). Principals have experienced a focus in individual schools on standards, high-stakes testing, and accountability (Tirozzi and Ferrandino 2001). At the elementary level, principals are working an average of 62 hours a week (Groff 2001). Schools have changed the roles of principals with regard to the school day. Principals are responsible for all the activities within the school environment, regardless of when the day starts or ends. Gerald Tirozzi, executive director of the National Association of Secondary School Principals, and Vincent Ferrandino, executive director of the National Association of Elementary School Principals, summarized the problem of the increasing diversity and complexity of principals' roles:

> The principal must be a legal expert, health and social services coordinator, fundraiser, public relations consultant, security officer, who is technologically savvy, diplomatic with top-notch managerial skills, whose most important duty is the implementation of instructional programs, curricula, pedagogical practice, and assessment models (Tirozzi and Ferrandino 2001).

Because of the changing responsibilities of principals, researchers have documented that the shortage of qualified principals is a growing concern. In a three-year study in the spring of 2000, researchers with the Association of California School Administrators reported that principals are resigning from their positions at younger ages because of stress and increased job responsibilities and accountability requirements. Researchers in 2001 found that in Washington, 15 percent of the principals had retired or resigned at the end of the 1999–2000 school year. In Vermont, the situation was worse; 50 percent of principals had retired or resigned. In New York City, 163 schools began the 1999–2000 school year with interim principals (Groff 2001). In 2002, 42 percent of the school districts in the United States did not have qualified candidates for the principalship. Because of the lack of qualified candidates in Washington state, researchers reported that 30 principals had to be "recruited" from retirement to fill positions temporarily at both the elementary and high school levels (Copland 2001). The Department of Labor reported in the same year that 40 percent of over 90,000 principals were almost at retirement age, creating a major concern about the principal shortage (US Bureau of Labor Statistics, 2002). Yet the school population continues to increase, and the demand for principals in the job market adds even more stress (Bloom and Krovetz 2001). Not surprisingly, researchers reported that the candidate pool for open positions is not limited but also lacking in preparation for the increased job responsibilities (Kerrins, Johnstone, and Cushing 2001; Groff 2001). Because of the significant change in the principals' roles, the need for master principals who possess adaptive skills for leading the ever-changing school environment is most important.

During this decade and for years to come, the complexity and stress as a leader because of the expectations will continue to become more demanding (Peterson and Kelly 2001; Goodwin 2004). In a 2000–2001 national survey of over 400 high school principals, the increased expectations for the future were identified as greater accountability for students' test scores, discipline problems, dropout rates, safety, and social and economic issues.

Promoting Character Education: A Model Staff Development Plan for
Beginning Principals

Activity	Assessment/Demonstration of Knowledge
Encourage staff to read extensively about new character education models and how to implement them in the classrooms examples: teaching literature, current events, and issues that deal with moral issues	Presentation to faculty
Attend national conferences on character education	Reflective journals
Using case study journals and/or books, respond to scenarios/vignettes that deal with integrity and ethics	Discussion of scenarios/vignettes with administrative team
Work with stakeholders to develop or update a code of ethics for the school community	Survey to assess awareness of standards
Develop school discipline protocols that promote respect, caring, and responsibility	Fewer discipline problems
Develop guidelines for physical education curriculum that emphasize fairness, self-discipline, and conflict resolution	Improved climate and culture of sportsmanship

In the social realm, principals will find it necessary to be models, leading, instructing, and motivating teachers, parents, and students to accept the challenges of today and tomorrow. The moral and ethical principal is one who values himself and others and achieves to the greatest heights to which he aspires. This person values the achievements of others as well and contributes to the success of the school community and later to society as a whole. The integration of good moral character produces the empathetic learner who wants the best for society and wants to contribute to that success.

The Challenge

Achieving a moral and ethical learning environment begins with the principal as the instructional leader of the school. The moral school leader enhances the success of all students and teachers by modeling integrity, a sense of fairness, and behaving in an ethical manner. The ethical instructional leader attempts to hire the best moral teachers and encourages an atmosphere that creates a climate for teaching and integrating moral values in every student.

As the instructional leader in the school, the principal creates a program of discipline that is based on moral values and helps students to make good choices. The curriculum provides for problem solving in areas of moral development, both formally and informally. A safe learning environment is created to encourage empathy and caring in the school community. School leaders and staff, to ensure that students are treated with dignity and respect, must also model values that are desired among and for students. One goal of the school community should be to nurture contributing members for a more tolerant community.

Suggested Readings

Blackburn, S. 2001. *Being Good: An Introduction to Ethics*. New York: Oxford University Press.

Gardner, H., W. Damon, and M. Csikszentmihalyi. 2001. *Good Work: When Excellence and Ethics Meet*. New York: Basic Books.

Sergiovanni, T. J. 1992. *Moral Leadership: Getting to the Heart of School Improvement*. New York: Jossey-Bass Education Series.

Sizer, N. F., and T. R. Sizer. 1999. *The Children Are Watching: School and the Moral Character*. Boston: Beacon Press.

Suggested Activities

These could be completed as small or large group discussions, online chat discussions facilitated by the professor, or individual written assignments.

1. Describe the functions of the principal as an instructional leader in the development of character education in the schools.

2. Describe the principal as a moral leader in the community.

3. Discuss whether moral values of school leaders are innate or learned and defend your position.

4. Describe several concrete ways that curriculum in preparation programs for aspiring school leaders may be employed to teach good morals and

develop character as described by the indicators for ISLLC/ELCC Standard 5.

5. Discuss the importance of integrity, fairness, and ethics on the part of the principal.

6. How might the principal encourage teaching good morals and ethics in staff development sessions?

7. How do the demands of accountability laws impact the integrity, fairness, and ethics of a school leader?

MAJOR CHAPTER ASSIGNMENT

1. Either individually or in small groups, develop a personal code of ethics for your reference point to implement ISLLC/ELCC Standard 5 as a school leader.

2. Complete a brief reflection about the material in Chapter 5 in your reflection journal.

3. Using the case study *The Quandary* by Dr. Stanley S. Schainker, below, identify the issues as they relate to ethics, fairness, and integrity, and write a brief concept paper describing how you would use the major concepts in Chapter 6 to address those issues. (This activity could also be a small-group, cooperative project.)

The Quandary

by
Stanley A. Schainker, University of North Carolina at
Chapel Hill (with permission)

Hattie Powel, an elected representative serving on the Big Rock Middle School's site-based management team (SBMT) and one of three assistant principals of the school, was in a quandary. The local Businessmen's Club has given the school $12,000 "to use on any single project that will benefit the school." The responsibility for making the decision has fallen into the collective lap of the 11-person SBMT consisting of one administrator (Hattie), four teachers, four parents, and two students. The team is to vote this afternoon on one of four projects under consideration for funding. The projects being considered are:

1. Giving classroom teachers approximately $250 each to purchase instructional supplies.

2. Establishing a Black Pride Club that would meet after school and on Saturdays for tutoring assistance and cultural activities (the school has 150 African-American students in a student body of 600).

3. Purchasing a new electronic scoreboard for the gymnasium.

4. Purchasing for the school media center a 400-book collection that celebrates the trials, tribulations, triumphs, and contributions of African-Americans throughout the history of the United States.

Hattie, one of six African-American certified staff in the school, was the media specialist there for seven years prior to being appointed an assistant principal this year. Because she knew the library was inadequate when it came to books that focused on black history, she personally favored this project for funding.

However, other factors made her decision difficult. Eighty percent of the school's teachers favored giving each teacher money for classroom supplies. Three of Hattie's black colleagues on the faculty urged her to support funding for a Black Pride Club. A number of ministers of local African-American churches and other community leaders also contacted her to ask her to support this club. Hattie has talked with the principal, for whom she has had much respect, and he asked her to support a new scoreboard. He said it would benefit all students, serve as a visible and permanent improvement to the school, and be utilized by a wide range of people, since the gym was used for adult basketball and exercise classes. In addition, the president of the Businessmen's Club (who happens to be the CEO of the community's largest employer) called the principal to urge funding of the scoreboard for "his son's basketball team."

Hattie also knows from conversations with them that the two student members of the SBMT prefer the scoreboard first and the library collection second. She believes three of the four parent members support giving teachers supply money and the fourth parent (a white male) supports the scoreboard. What will Hattie do?

INDIVIDUAL REACTION

In the schools today, acting with integrity, fairly and ethically while promoting the success of all students, may appear to be difficult. Explain how in this rapidly changing society, you as a future principal will always act with integrity, fairly and ethically.

What will be your moral compass?

Write out your belief system as related to these essential skills.

6

Standard Six: Understanding, Responding to, and Influencing the Larger Contexts as an Essential of Leadership Development

Principals must live with paradox: they must have a sense of urgency about improving their schools balanced by the patience to sustain them for the long haul. They must focus on the future but remain grounded in today. They must see the big picture while maintaining a close focus on details. They must be strong leaders who give away power to others.

—Richard DuFour (1999)

ISLLC Standard 6	ELCC Standard 6
A school administrator is an educational leader who promotes the success of all students by understanding, responding to, and influencing the larger political, social, economic, legal, and cultural context.	*Candidates who complete the program are educational leaders who have the knowledge and ability to promote the success of all students by understanding, responding to, and influencing the larger political, social, economic, legal, and cultural context.*

In America today, school administrators have become the linchpins for maintaining the quality of schools and students. Principals are representative change agents who transform schools into places of learning and growth. Responding to the intricate webs of educational reform, principals' roles are continually evolving and changing. Through the progression of the accountability movement that began with the publication of *A Nation at Risk* (1983) and *Leaders for America's Schools* (1987), students, teachers, and administrators are held accountable for their performance through standards.

Administrators must be responsive to the continually shifting trends in society, and ISLLC Standard 6 specifically addresses these issues. As school leaders, principals will have the greatest capacity to transform schools from bureaucratic machines into democratic entities. The political, social, economic, legal, and cultural issues from society will continue to affect schools. The degree and impact will depend upon the education leader's decisions.

Implications for Effective School Leadership

As transformational leaders focusing on school change and improvement, school principals have an enormously multifaceted job. Acting as constant catalysts for change, administrators must balance the needs of the students and teachers in the school with the demands and initiatives of the school district, school board, and larger community. Although the role of instruction is paramount in schools, there are influences impacting the education of students beyond the classroom.

Standard 6 (Council of Chief State School Officers 1996) specifically states "a school administrator is an educational leader who promotes the success of all students by understanding, responding to, and influencing the larger political, social, economic, legal, and cultural contexts" (p. 20). The Consortium clearly included the outside factors as impacting and influencing the operations and leadership in a school. Schools are microcosms of society and reflect the shifts and trends of the larger, democratic populace. The responsive leader anticipates conflicts and has appropriate management strategies and policies in place so the learning community of the school is not adversely disrupted (McCall 1994).

There are four factors that can leave a profound impression on schools and leaders: financial issues, politics, the law, and the societal milieu within which a school functions. Given budget crises occurring in numerous states, the issue of finance is particularly relevant. Public schools have the security of public funding, but that sense of certainty is quickly eroding as financial cuts gouge deeply into school district budgets. Schools are asked to run on shoestring budgets, cutting everything from after-school programs to textbooks to assistant principals. As a result, building principals must be extremely cautious and vigilant with funding; in times of economic uncertainty, the public will scrutinize school budgets and spending closely. Administrators must be financially savvy within the school, using resources "in-house" and allocating the bulk of the funding to effective instructional methods (Odden 2001).

Public schools are state entities and consequently are largely governed by political influence (Bracey 2001). The accountability movement, mandatory testing requirements for students and teachers, and federal legislation all fall under the auspices of politics. The adept school leader is aware of potential political influences on schools and makes appropriate strategies and plans when implementation of mandates must occur. The bureaucratic wheel of government serves to benefit and sometimes hinder education. A principal must have ongoing dialogue with diverse stakeholders within the school community to advocate beneficial educational policies and legislation. Schools are political animals, and administrators must recognize the political culture of the community (Fowler 2000). To neglect this beast is to invite disaster.

The governance of schools falls under either the state constitution or state statutes. These laws guide the actions of school administrators and school personnel. Prudent administrators realize that the law is forever evolving and changing; consequently, principals must be critically aware of updates in case law, state statutes, federal legislation, and opinions of lawmakers. School leaders who follow the law have traditionally served to ensure equitable, fair, and just treatment for all students; however, lawsuits and liability issues should alert school leaders of potential hazards (Joyce 2000). Administrators must know the law and apprise faculty and staff of the legal system functions and current law cases.

Societal ills have been historically commonplace in schools. As shifts in societal beliefs and ideals take place, the school community is quite often called upon to deal with the transgressions of the larger society. If too many teenagers become pregnant or if influential and vocal community members perceive the morals of students to be deteriorating, schools must teach sex education. However, community groups may have culture clashes about what specifically should be taught—abstinence or birth control, same-sex marriage or traditional family structure, sexual orientation, etc., etc. If American students do not perform well on standardized tests in comparison with other countries, schools must institute mandatory standards and testing. If students are less honest and responsible than previous generations, schools need to develop character education programs. A calculated pattern begins to emerge—schools must "fix all of society's ills."

School leaders are trapped in the unenviable position of instituting changes within the school that the faculty may not be trained or equipped to handle effectively. The roles of schools, teachers, and administrators have been transformed into that of caregiver, counselor, and moral agent when dealing with major changes in the society. Administrators must be careful to balance the needs of the students in the school—student learning, first and foremost—with the societal goals of schooling (Howe and Townsend 2000). Even when school staffs are equipped to assist families and deal with problems, the school community cannot handle every crisis for every family every day. There is neither enough time in the day, enough resources, nor enough expertise in the school for the faculty and staff to be everything to everybody all the time. It is the principal's responsibility to help staff determine what can realistically be accomplished, when to reach out to other agencies, and when a problem is simply beyond the capacity of the school to solve.

Faculty Improvement

A redefined role for school faculties and staff is included in the renaissance of American education. School faculties can be ideal professionals if they are committed to the best interests of children. In an age of accountability, teachers, assistants, and leaders must persevere against dwindling budgets, increasing political pressures to perform, a plethora of legal mandates, and an influx of abdicated societal and parental responsibilities. Despite the mounting obstacles to continual growth, innovative administrators find ways and means to provide learning opportunities for students.

To help implement the latest political reform efforts or courses aimed at curing the most recent societal ills, building principals can become extremely creative in their approaches to faculty development. First, administrators should look within the walls of the school for experts on given topics and use those individuals to conduct the necessary training and initiations (Queen and Algozzine 2007a). This cost-efficient method allows various staff members to "showcase" talents. Employing the services of the local university is another strategy for professional learning opportunities. A myriad of experts at these institutions is available and offers resources to the public schools.

Partnerships with other social agencies should be explored and implemented. Formal procedures can be established so collaboration is an entity that comes into play as specific and regular routines for the benefit of truly meeting the needs of the "whole" child.

Expertise may also be obtained through the local school district. Central office personnel are specialists and are willing to help a school faculty with professional learning development. School districts are now beginning to offer leadership academies where administrators and teachers can take advantage of opportunities to build upon knowledge bases at no additional cost. Professional learning opportunities should be continuous, well planned, and should meet the needs of the practitioners.

Student Achievement in a Milieu of Accountability

The purpose of school is student learning; however, with the wave of reform efforts, budget crises, legal mandates, and accountability demands, the focus of schools can sometimes become blurred. The transformational leader who is responsive to such trends is aware of changes in the educational landscape.

Money does not always equate with a good education, although financial affluence can certainly buy more teachers and resources ("Quality counts," 2002).

There does seem to be a direct relationship with test scores and the median income of families in a community. Finances affect student achievement, but the committed and entrepreneurial administrator will not let that happen. Principals who are focused on instructional outcomes for students will not let financial issues negatively impact student learning. They will find grants, partner with businesses, plead for more resources from fiscal authorities, commit to fund raisers, oversee spending practices closely.

The current accountability movement initiated by politicians is affecting students by demanding additional performances and tests that must be mastered to earn course credit and a high school diploma. Although the standards can become prescriptive and monotonous, the stated purpose remains that every student should be held accountable to the school's high expectations. The intent of the accountability movement is that students will no longer be subject to disparities based on gender, race, socioeconomic status, or disability. This means directing resources and attention to the schools that need them the most. Theoretically, therefore, student achievement will not be marginalized for any political, legal, or fiscal issue.

High stakes accountability became even more high stakes with the passage of the No Child Left Behind Act (NCLB) during the first term of President George W. Bush. If a state had an accountability program prior to this, the program most likely needed major changes to comply with the new federal law. If the state did not have an accountability program in place, it would have to design and implement one very quickly. Accountability laws have resulted from strong political pressures, primarily from non-educators, with little to no stakeholder advocacy.

There are several political, social, cultural, and economic issues that need to be considered when implementing the NCLB Act or a state accountability program. Does a district need to measure student achievement growth or absolute performance? (NCLB requires absolute performance data, but many states have thus far required growth data.) How do state consequences for failing to meet the school's goals compare to consequences mandated under NCLB? What implications are there for implementing such a high-stakes accountability program for other important segments of schooling? What is the relationship between local control and state and federal accountability programs? How do accountability programs impact social justice and equity issues? What supports will be given to schools to assure they meet state and federal levels of success? How will school leaders attract highly qualified teachers to low-performing schools? How will teaching to the test be limited? How will curricula and pedagogy assure that higher-order thinking skills are an important part of the students' learning? How will cheating by students, teachers, and/or administrators be avoided? The answers must be considered when governing agencies are developing accountability policies, and, if not, must be open areas of discussion among faculty, students, community, and local school governance agencies.

Role of the Principal (ELLC Standard 6)

According to Murphy, Yff, and Shipman (2000), the principal's new role is characterized as being "empowering rather than controlling" (p. 19) and as "establishing meaning, rather than directing" (p. 19). "It is grounded more upon teaching than upon informing, more upon learning than upon knowing, and more upon modeling and clarifying values and beliefs than upon telling people what to do" (p. 19). The standards are in harmony with scientific theories that support the idea that sustainable improvements within social systems will occur only when sought and found by the stakeholders themselves. Senge and colleagues (2000) advocate the same idea, suggesting that we stop using the bureaucratic, machine-like model for schools and start viewing them as what they are: living systems. The fundamental distinction is that "living systems are self-made while machines are made by others" (p. 53). Similarly, Ubben, Hughes, and Norris (2001) use the brain metaphor to describe a school's contextual framework. The brain metaphor adds an "important dimension of thinking/learning organization. In this context, great emphasis is on shared knowledge and understandings, collaboration, and inquiry" (p. 185).

Leader as Decision Maker

The principal's most important responsibility is to hire highly qualified and competent classroom teachers who are capable of achieving the school's vision, mission, and goals. The principal's most important activity is to make sound, high-quality decisions that will benefit the school learning community (Lyons 2002). The primary purpose of schooling is student learning; although heavily influenced at times by political, legal, and financial forces, the leader must make decisions that facilitate positive learning outcomes. Principals are barraged on a daily basis to yield decisions that will affect various stakeholders in the school; the knowledgeable school leader is able to render a decision that is thoroughly investigated, ethical, fair, and free from personal bias (Green 2001).

When contemplating decisions, the school leader must understand the political, social, economic, legal, and cultural implications and responds by using an assortment of decision-making processes and strategies. Ubben, Hughes, and Norris (2001) contend that "to achieve good decisions, it is necessary to engage in problem analysis and select the best decision process." The quality of the decision is as crucial as the method employed to arrive at that decision. Although a multitude of decision-making processes is available to leaders, the Maier Model is exemplary because of its simplicity in design and feasibility in application.

The Maier Model, developed by Maier and Verser (1982), incorporates the two essential components necessary to consider when rendering a decision: quality and acceptance. The quality decision involves impartial judgments that center on accomplishing organizational goals and sustaining control. The

Figure 6.1
The Maier Model.

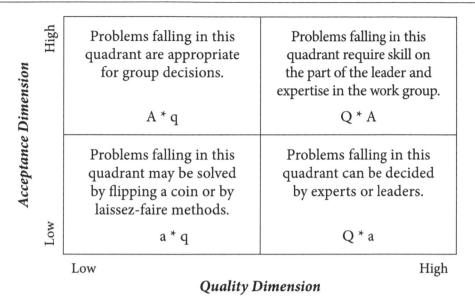

Source: Maier, N. R. F., and G. C. Verser. 1982. Psychology in Industrial Organizations, 5th ed. Boston: Houghton-Mifflin.

acceptance decision is the center of the commitment levels of subordinates. Figure 6.1 illustrates the quadrants involved in the Maier model. As depicted, the higher the level of quality and the lower the level of acceptance, school leaders without staff input or involvement may make decisions. Principals need to utilize consensus techniques, site-based management strategies, and personal expertise to elicit the best decisions. By employing the model when making decisions, administrators are destined to assess the quality and acceptance levels needed to arrive at a decision that maximizes the benefits for all affected. How does a principal determine which quadrant a problem falls into?

The ability to make sound, high-quality judgments and decisions that will prove to be beneficial over time is tremendously important; leadership behavior is intricately tied to arriving at prudent decisions. The researchers for *The Iowa Studies* (1939) proved influential in shaping the practices and behaviors of school administrators. Though more than 60 years have passed since the initial study, the researchers ascertained valuable leadership behavior traits that contribute to overall school success.

Lewin, Lippitt, and White (1939) reported three general categories of leadership: authoritarian, laissez-faire, and democratic. The authoritarian leaders were doctoral candidates who permitted no faculty input when making decisions; in contrast, the laissez-faire leaders allowed the faculty absolute freedom to arrive at decisions, which meant no recognizable leadership existed. Democratic leadership behaviors included group decision making, open communication, and encouragement to make suggestions for needed improvements. Subordinates in the study overwhelmingly preferred the behaviors demonstrated by democratic leaders.

The authors of *The Iowa Studies* have retrospectively confirmed modern practices that are widely respected today as essential leadership traits for successful administrators. By blending a sound model for decision making and the characteristics of a democratic leader, a principal becomes more capable of responding to and influencing the diverse needs of the learning community. There can be no substitute for sound judgment. The decision-making process is a core activity of school leaders, and the implications for unjust and unwise decisions can be far-reaching.

Leader as Conflict Manager

As with any modern organization where values, beliefs, and practices are vying for prominence, conflict is inevitable. Such is the case in all public schools. Conflict naturally occurs in schools because individuals are meshed into a collective entity, working toward a common goal (Green 2001). Competing reform efforts stemming from political, legal, social, and economic issues compound the already knotted existence of conflict in schools. As educational leaders, however, principals must ". . . have a knowledge and understanding of models and strategies of change and conflict resolution" (Council of Chief State School Officers, 1996).

The three most common areas of conflict are competition for scarce resources, a desire for autonomy, and divergence in goals (Green 2001). Conflicts among individuals, groups, teams, grades, or even departments can result in either destructive or productive behavior. However, once a conflict has been identified, the role of the principal shifts from leader to facilitator, trainer, and counselor. Efforts to solve conflict situations require the school leader to summon skill, knowledge, and tact. Green (2001) identifies five approaches to managing the conflict: avoidance, compromising, bargaining, power struggle, and problem solving. Each has value in particular conflict situations. A school leader, might choose avoidance when the conflict issue is of minimal importance and there is a desire for peaceful coexistence. Compromise may be an effective strategy when maintaining positive interpersonal relationships is a priority. If there is a moderate concern over both the task and the relationship involved, bargaining might be the strategy to employ to level the field. On the other hand, the power struggle method to conflict resolution involves a focus on the task that needs to be completed, not on relationships. Utilizing the problem-solving approach includes a collaborative effort to arrive at the best possible solution.

Six Steps to Effective Conflict Management

1. *Define the problem.* Avoid the blame game. Try to identify both persons' view of the conflict. Most likely, there will always be two sides to a story with each side honestly believing it is in the right. Sometimes, it is possible that both are correct, and the participants are simply giving different accounts of the same situation. This step will take time and patience. Listen. Do not make judgments. Consider that differences in culture may affect one's view or understanding. Allow the feelings to flow, even the inevitable anger and defensiveness. Before moving to the next steps, be sure all parties to the conflict agree on the definition of the problem.

2. *Brainstorm possible solutions.* Brainstorming by definition allows open discussion of ideas with no critiquing. All ideas should be treated with respect. This process will also take time. Constantly refer back to the statement of the problem. When several possible solutions are generated, then start a process of evaluating them and move to step three.

3. *Evaluate the possible solutions generated in step 2.* This will include a certain level of trust, critical thinking, and an open mind to change and compromise. This step may even create some additional solutions that were not considered during step two.

4. *Participants mutually agree to attempt one of the solutions identified in the earlier steps.* If all participants are not firmly committed to a sincere attempt to implement the solution, it will not work.

5. *Act on the agreed-upon solution.* The goal in this step is not to seek consequences for unsuccessful implementation, but rather to identify who does what and when.

6. *Keep a watchful eye on how the solution is implemented until the conflict is totally resolved.* It is acceptable to make changes during this phase, if all participants agree. All should know ahead of initial implementation that changes could be made if mutual agreement is reached. To do this will require honest communications among the parties.

If processed effectively, conflict can be healthy for the organization and lead to new and useful resolutions. Careful identification of the problem, thorough analysis of the possible solutions, and a direct approach to managing the conflict will allow teachers, students, and school leaders to focus on the purpose of schools—learning. Conflicts should not be ignored or allowed to grow and fester.

Leader as Change Agent

As previously stated, innovation and change are key words in a principal's vocabulary. As the leader of the learning community and likely initiator of change, the administrator must have knowledge and understanding of the change process for systems, organizations, and individuals (Council of Chief State School Officers 1996). Studies by Brickell (1964) and Griffiths (1963) found that the single most influential change agents in school systems are either principals or superintendents. The competent educational leader is also aware of "the political, social, cultural, and economic systems and processes that impact schools" (Council of Chief State School Officers 1996).

Gordon Lippett, in a presentation to school principals in the Montgomery County Public Schools in Maryland in the 1970s, identified several reasons why people resist change. We believe these still hold true in the 21st century.

- ◆ Goals and purposes are unclear.
- ◆ Stakeholders are not involved.
- ◆ The change is promoted through personal appeal.
- ◆ Group norms (school culture) are ignored.
- ◆ Inadequate communications.
- ◆ Fear of failure.
- ◆ Inadequate rewards.
- ◆ Lack of trust in the change agent.
- ◆ Satisfaction with the status quo.
- ◆ Lack of insight and security of the part of the school leader.

According to Green (2001), change occurs when a school leader endeavors to modify the behavior, program, purpose, or structure of elements within the school. The school personnel must be committed to student learning and should continually seek to improve the environment of the learning community. Change can be both beneficial and disruptive. Leaders and the school faculty must become active participants in the change process. Earlier, Johnson (1970) also indicated that change involves a collaborative effort that includes mutual determination of goals and equal opportunities to exert influence. Such a relationship is very clearly necessary to generate trust and overcome inevitable resistance to change.

We believe that principals who encounter resistance to change should pay close heed to seven key areas:

1. *Involvement*. If members of an organization are not deeply involved from the very beginning of a change effort, they will resist the proposed change. They will simply be more inclined to support change when they have an

active part in the planning rather than just implementing someone else's plan. Chung (1970) advocates teacher-centered leadership that gives teachers a strong voice in decision making. The implications are clear. If school leaders want to be effective change agents, they must adopt a collaborative process with stakeholders.

2. *Information.* New and best practices in education do not happen unless teachers know about them. However, school leaders who direct teachers to implement the innovation du jour with little or no screening, sorting, or research simply invite resistance. The leader and the leadership team must develop procedures for communication and dissemination of available literature for any proposed change. Find a meaningful, efficient, and nonthreatening way to share information with already very busy and committed teachers.

3. *Advocacy and feedback.* No change will be successful without support of the top-level administrators in a system, including the central office and the principal. If the change is one suggested by central office leaders, the principal's behavior and attitude toward the proposed change will indicate to the teachers and community how seriously they should take the proposal. Recognition of how teachers are coping with a change and providing frequent and easy avenues for feedback are critical.

4. *Visitations.* (Not a spiritual happening, but perhaps similar in some ways!) To help teachers, in particular, overcome resistance to the proposed change, send them to visit other schools that have successfully implanted a similar program. Plan the visits with specific goals about the knowledge, ideas, and concepts to be gained. Follow up with a collaborative analysis of what the visiting teachers saw and heard, both positive and negative. Allow plenty of time for visitations, reading, discussion, attendance at conferences, and participation in worthwhile workshops. Between disseminating information about a new idea and implementing the concept, let people have time to understand it. Haste breeds resistance; deliberation paves the way for success.

5. *Skills and professional development.* Another potential barrier to change is lack of necessary skills by those expected to implement the innovation. Professional development must be provided in sufficient quantity and quality in order to see any substantive change in role expectations and behaviors.

6. *Resources.* The implementation team should design systems to assure successful implementation, support during implementation, and sustaining the change once it has been institutionalized. Doing this could affect personnel, budget, and/or time. It may necessitate reallocation of resources from established programs. It may even necessitate elimination of some programs that have been in place but are no longer relevant to the school's goals.

As educational leaders in the various levels of public schools, principals can create a school climate that is receptive to change. Green (2001) identifies eight actions that build a capacity for change:

1. Establishing effective lines of communication between the school leader and the community.
2. Securing community support for the change concept.
3. Acquiring expertise in the new program concept.
4. Driving fear out of the school.
5. Working out collective bargaining regulations that facilitate change.
6. Acquiring necessary approvals from the state department of education.
7. Identifying sources of the necessary resources.
8. Utilizing effective change strategies.

Ubben, Hughes, and Norris (2001) identify two basic strategic approaches to change: directive and participatory. In directive decision making, the school leader simply identifies the directions, purpose, and restrictions for those parties responsible for implementing the change. The participatory decision-making model for change is more compatible with the desired democratic leadership behaviors. With the participatory approach, the leader gives all members of the school community the opportunity to discuss and implement the desired changes. Like the authors of the ISLLC Standards, we specifically endorse the participatory approach, indicating "the administrator believes in, values, and is committed to the involvement of . . . other stakeholders in school decision-making processes" (ISLLC 1996).

Even though reformers would like change in schools to be immediate, the reality is that change occurs incrementally (Tyack and Cuban 1995). A school leader can minimize the stress and frustration associated with change by adopting a democratic approach. The democratic leader fosters a supportive and cooperative environment that is highly compatible with the modern organizational structures (Lunenburg and Ornstein 2000). Change is both constant and inevitable, but educational leaders realize that change can become synonymous with improvement—a concept that can function to facilitate student learning.

Healthy organizations are open to and accepting of change. Ideally, it is the school leadership team that launches and supports openness to new ideas. Organized thinking and planning about specific objectives related to a school's improvement plans should lead to concrete conceptualization of worthwhile changes. Successful implementation of meaningful change will lead to a culture of perpetual self-renewal in a school.

Table 6.2

Understanding, Responding to, and Influencing the Larger Political, Social, Economic, Legal, and Cultural Context: A Model Staff Development Plan for Beginning Principals

Activity	Assessment/Demonstration of Knowledge
Work to cultivate a mentor relationship with established educational leader	Formal and informal observations by mentor
Attend national conferences on political, social, economic, legal, and cultural issues related to the principalship	Reflective journals
Participate in activities/seminars for first-year principal cohort at the district level	Attendance and active participation and at activities/seminars
Using case study journals and/or books, respond to scenarios/vignettes that deal with responding to external influences	Discussion of scenarios/vignettes with administrative team
Attend law conferences and law updates given by the school district	No reported incidents involving legal situations
Design and distribute surveys to assess the political, social, and cultural climates of the school	Develop professional learning opportunities for faculty which address need areas
Attend workshops on conflict management	Decreased incidents of conflict within the school
Receive training on how to effectively run meetings	Evaluation rubrics completed by faculty indicating satisfaction with meetings and agendas
Utilize several decision-making strategies and processes to make quality decisions	Dialogue with stakeholders in the school about climate and culture
Use positive verbal and written communication with faculty, students, parents, and community	Fewer complaints lodged at the district office

The Challenge

The educational leaders in America have the responsibility of ensuring teacher performance and student success. As responsive educational leaders, principals must "promote the success of all students by understanding, responding to, and influencing the larger political, social, economic, legal, and cultural contexts" (ISLLC 1996). These societal influences can either negatively or positively impact public schools. Transformational leaders will embrace the challenges stemming from society for the betterment of the learning community.

Suggested Readings

Goldberg, M. F. 2001. Leadership in education: Five commonalities. *Phi Delta Kappan 82*(10), 757–761.

Green, R. L. 2001. *Practicing the Art of Leadership: A Problem-Based Approach to Implementing the ISLLC Standards.* Upper Saddle River, NJ: Merrill/Prentice-Hall.

National Association of Elementary School Principals. 2001. *Leading Learning Communities: NAESP Standards for What Principals Should Know and Be Able to Do.* Alexandria, VA: Author.

National Center for Educational Statistics. 2001. *Selected Papers in School Finance, 2000–2001.* Washington, DC: United States Department of Education.

Suggested Activities

1. Questions for Class Discussion

Address these questions individually in writing, or in small groups, or as a whole class discussion, or online with monitoring and/or facilitation by the professor.

1. Explore the predominant themes of ISLLC and ELCC Standard 6 and how the concepts affect the actions of a principal.

2. Discuss the current educational reform movements and describe the potential impact on school leadership.

3. Brainstorm a list of possible alternative decision-making strategies to use with a school faculty.

4. What precautions could be instituted to ensure that quality decisions are made?

5. Why is the role of conflict manager so crucial for school leaders?

6. Create a graphic organizer of the actions that create an atmosphere conducive for change and then deliberate which action is the most critical for a principal to master.

7. What specific actions and/or responsibilities of the principal as described in Standard 6 could be correlated to student achievement?

2. Reflections: Complete a brief reflection about the material in Chapter 6 in your reflection journal.

3. Case Study: Using the case study *No Easy Way Out* by Dr. Stanley S. Schainker, below, identify the issues as they relate to political, social, economic, legal, and/or cultural context, and write a brief concept paper describing how you would use the major concepts in Chapter 6 to address those issues. (This activity could also be a small-group cooperative project.)

No Easy Way Out

by
Stanley A. Schainker, University of North Carolina at
Chapel Hill (with permission)

Phil Owens, the superintendent of the Tower Hill School District, had a problem. He never had faced a situation in which so much resistance had surfaced in reaction to a proposal. He knew that there was no easy way out.

Owens had been hired to provide leadership needed to take on the difficult issues associated with consolidating two districts. The previous year the former county school district (16,000 students, top 10 percent of state districts in terms of academic achievement, 80 percent white/20 percent African-American) had been merged with the former city school district (8,000 students, bottom 10 percent of state districts in terms of academic achievement, 80 percent African-American/20 percent white). The merger had been approved by a public referendum that passed by a mere 900 votes out of 30,000 votes cast.

The newly constituted board of education promised the community that a new student assignment plan would be implemented to significantly improve the racial makeup of all schools and to strengthen the quality of instructional programs for all students. Owens and his top-level staff have devoted the last six months to collecting information, listening to parental and staff concerns, and devising a plan to revamp the distribution of students among the district's schools. When he presented the report and recommendations to the school board and public two weeks ago, chaos erupted.

The following is a summary of the feedback received to date:

1. The four white board members have criticized the plan publicly for not being specific enough about how each school's educational program would be improved.

2. The three black board members have criticized the plan publicly for placing a disproportionate burden on black students to integrate the schools.

3. Powerful, veteran members of his own staff have told Owens privately how disappointed they are that a number of last-minute changes were made to the plan in response to political pressures. They advised him that these changes "have created inconsistencies that serve to undermine the overall integrity of the plan."

4. The Teachers' Association president issued a press release emphasizing that teachers need assurances that they would not be involuntarily reassigned. The president of the Association went on to say that teachers were feeling very uncomfortable about the changing expectations for them, most of which they feel unprepared to meet.

5. The executive board of the School-Based Administrators Association (principals and assistant principals) complained at the last board meeting that their input was basically ignored, and, in fact, they believe they had very little involvement in developing the instructional emphases for the proposed plan.

6. The president of the district's PTA board suggested that the public should have several options so citizens may engage in informed debate about the crucial issues that are impacting the community.

7. The local newspaper, while supporting the superintendent's proposal, urged that everything be slowed down so deliberations could be made about how to pay for implementation.

8. The chamber of commerce also called for a two-year moratorium on any changes in order to give adequate time for thorough and open discussion "among all people who will be impacted by the changes."

Owens knows the redistricting issue must be addressed. He also knows there will be organized resistance. His reputation and future job prospects depend on satisfactory resolution of this issue. There is quite simply no easy way out!

MAJOR CHAPTER ASSIGNMENT

1. Divide the class into two groups, with one group supporting and one group opposing the No Child Left Behind Act. Using political, social, economic, legal, and cultural justifications, have each group present its position and rationale.

2. Students should conduct an interview with a high-level elected official from their district (county commissioner, board member, state legislator, etc.) about how they are influenced in their decision making by the political, social, economic, legal, and cultural factors in the community. Either written or oral reports should be completed summarizing the interview statements.

REACTION

Explain how a principal or future principal can deal with the larger educational context. List and discuss ten actual experiences that you have faced or may face as a principal and discuss in small groups the best ways to handle each.

7

Standard Seven: Effective Practice as an Essential of Leadership Development

It has been said that the principalship was conceived in a halo of chalk dust.

—L. Joseph Matthews and Gary M. Crow (2003)

ELCC Standard 7
The internship provides significant opportunities for candidates to synthesize and apply the knowledge and practice and develop the skills identified in Standards 1 through 6 through substantial, sustained, standards-based work in real settings, planned and guided cooperatively by the institution and school district personnel for graduate credit.

In developing the ISLLC Standards, the Interstate School Leaders Licensure Consortium aimed to develop leadership standards aligned "to the goal of improved student learning imbedded in language that reflects the real-world environment of principals" (Trends, 1992). The Educational Leadership Constituent Council embraced the six ISLLC Standards and added a seventh that focuses on the internship experience as an essential element of graduate education for school leaders. The intent of the internship is to provide real-world experiences that augment academic knowledge and expand skills, positioning future educational administrators to lead with confidence and strength.

In this chapter, we link ELCC Standard 7 to the evolution of the principal's role in the school environment. We outline the essential knowledge for school leaders that the standard encompasses. Finally, we offer feedback from individuals reflecting on the internship experience.

The Principal's Role

In a changing political, social, economic, legal, and cultural climate, expectations for administrative roles and preparation programs are under increased scrutiny. Aspiring principals can no longer rely solely on academic knowledge in order to be effective leaders. The six linked ISLLC and ELCC Standards and the ELCC internship model aimed to equip future leadership candidates with the ability to successfully perform in roles that continue to increase in complexity.

Although the physical appearance of schools has not changed a good deal in recent decades, society and the job market have changed significantly in just the last 20 years. Society has undergone a demographic shift. Traditional families represent but one facet of a complicated mosaic, and minority students with limited English proficiency continue to enroll in schools in increased numbers. Technological forces such as the Internet have created a link to global influences. These influences on society reflect a demand for more active learning strategies for students. In response, school leaders must focus on human resources to achieve success for all students. They must facilitate change by leading the way to teacher and student empowerment. They must strive to provide success for all students in an environment of increasing complexity.

"Connections between the academic and practice arms of the profession and about appropriate anchoring values are all highlighted in the evolutionary tapestry of principal preparation" (Murphy 1998). Early schools were simplistic in structure. Teachers advanced to leadership roles with no formal training, relying instead on common sense, intrinsic abilities, and classroom experience.

"American schools during the seventeenth and eighteenth centuries were mostly private or church institutions" (Matthews and Crow 2003). Thomas Jefferson was one of the first to address the demand for public education in America in the early 1800s. His proposal for free public education at the state's expense was not well accepted. Wealthy taxpayers protested the idea of their tax dollars used to educate society's children. Jefferson's proposals, not adopted at this time, would later lead others to draw the same conclusions. Decades later, building on Jefferson's ideas, Horace Mann in Massachusetts and Henry Barnard in Connecticut initiated the public school movement referred to as the *common school movement* (Matthews and Crow 2003).

First references to the term *principal* appeared in Horace Mann's 1841 report to the Massachusetts School Board. As public schools flourished, pupil and staff populations grew. With the growth was the need for one individual to take responsibility for the administrative duties in a school. Horace Mann used the term in this report to indicate the primary or principal teacher filling this role within the school environment (Matthews and Crow 2003).

In 1839, The Common School Teacher's Association made a request to the Cincinnati Board of Education to establish the necessary duties of the principal teacher (Matthews and Crow 2003). Although the wording may be different, many of the principals' responsibilities determined in 1839 resemble duties performed by principals of today:

- Function as head master.
- Regulate classes and course of instruction of all pupils.
- Discover defects in the school and apply remedies, if unable to remedy conditions make the defects known to trustees of ward or districts.
- Give instruction to his assistants.
- Classify pupils.
- Safeguard schoolhouses and furniture.
- Keep the school clean.
- Refrain from impairing the standing of assistants, especially in the eyes of their pupils.
- Require the cooperation of his assistants (Matthews and Crow 2003).

Over time, the principal's role has changed into a "product influenced by various interacting elements" (Matthews and Crow 2003). Molded by social and cultural forces, the principal's role is changing as schools and society direct. "Whatever the source, and whatever the reason, educational leaders are being targeted as the group most responsible for accomplishing any accountability theme, from kindergarten through college." Mattocks and Drake (2001) state that this requirement affects the mode of current educational leaders and has serious implications for the training of future leaders in education (p. 15). "Charter schools, vouchers, decentralized governance, standardized testing, accountability, and youth social issues have provoked new pressures that no principal could have anticipated a decade ago" (Matthews and Crow 2003).

Graduate programs that focus on the preparation of visionary school leaders able to deal with the educational, social, and political complexities facing communities must be restructured to address these areas and be developed in conjunction with established standards. Standards such as the ISLLC Standards developed by professional organizations relate to what scholars have researched and written about in relationship to the school leader. These standards should lead to the development of visionary school leaders through the training of higher education institutions and school systems.

There are many examples in the history of educational leadership of attempts to change preparation programs. "To prepare educational leaders for the numerous settings and changing requirements is not an easy business" (Young and Peterson 2002). One of the problems identified with preparatory programs is the lack of connection between teachings at the university and what practitioners need to do in their schools. Some programs ignore the "basic understanding of how people learn and master competencies required for effective leadership" (Hoachlander, Sikora, & Horn, 2003). Students learn by doing. In order to learn to lead, aspiring principals need opportunities to bridge the gap from theory to practice. School leaders can no longer work solely as managers of facilities and disciplinarians. Formal education programs, operated by universities, must prepare principals for complex educational situations with greater responsibility for working with diverse communities and parents.

Essential Knowledge for School Leaders

The internship for aspiring principals is a key component in the leadership model for new principals. We strongly agree with the quote of our coauthor, Dr. Shipman: "An environment of political, social, and economic change is shaping the direction for schools and school leadership." (Speech to Principal Fellows Group, UNCC, 2003). In order to provide realistic training ground for prospective principals, they must fully experience the daily workings of the leadership role. Traditional managerial roles will no longer suffice in an environment of societal and educational changes based on diversity needs, accountability standards, and public expectations. Legislative issues have transformed the right to a basic education into one viewed by the public as an entitlement. All of these factors play a major part in the need for strong leaders with extensive on-the-job training. Recommendations from professional organizations support the need for internship components in addition to the university training for principal preparation programs.

ELCC Standard 7 addresses the importance of structured, sustained, and Standards-based experiences in authentic settings. The internship is defined as the process and the product that results from applying the knowledge and skills described in Standards 1 through 6 in a workplace environment. Application of Standards-based knowledge, skills, and research in real settings over time is critical aspect of any institutional program. The provision of graduate credit allows institutions to underscore the importance of this activity.

Leaders should be knowledgeable in the following areas: specific internship experiences, preparing for the first year as a principal, the principal as staff development leader, and the principal as leader for student achievement.

Specific internship experiences. For students who are preparing to become principals, the internship is a valuable learning experience. It can provide many opportunities for the intern to grow as a school leader. The internship allows the student to transfer the knowledge and skills learned in the university classroom to the schoolhouse. When beginning the internship experience, it is important that both the intern and the supervising administrator understand the types of experiences that the intern will need to have. Some of those experiences might include curriculum, dealing with disciplinary issues, understanding budgets and finances, personnel evaluations and decisions, exceptional children's issues, buses, athletics, and public relations. There may also be other items specific to individual schools or grade configurations.

Preparing for the first year as a principal. The first year as a school administrator can be both challenging and stressful. First-year principals are often put into situations where they must simply sink or swim. They can lack professional support and may face faculties that are distrusting of them. Rooney (2000) gives several tips to first-year principals as they prepare for their first principalship:

- Respect the past with its heroes, heroines, icons, and rituals.
- Meet each teacher and department chair.
- Locate the power.
- Keep the central office informed.
- Find friends and mentors among your colleagues.
- When in doubt, keep still.
- Take care of yourself physically, emotionally, professionally, and spiritually.
- Continue to learn by reading, attending professional meetings, and conversing with professional friends.
- Pick your battles.

Principals as staff development leaders. The primary function of any principal is to serve as the instructional leader within the school. In this capacity, you are responsible for the instruction for both students and staff. Staff development serves a critical role in helping both principals and teachers increase their content knowledge and their understanding of effective teaching practices. You can exercise this leadership in two ways. One is to plan staff development for teachers that meets their needs and the needs of the school. Teachers should have an active role in discussions concerning the staff development that will be taking place, and you should use concrete data to ascertain what areas within the school to address. Professional development should also allow teachers the chance to practice and reflect on what they learn, and it should be sustained over time, rather than a one-day workshop.

A second way that principals can serve as staff development leader is by being an active participant in staff development. Effective principals realize that it is just as important for them to be continuously learning and growing as it is for their teachers.

Principals as leaders for student achievement. As an instructional leader, your greatest responsibility is to promote student achievement. In essence, this is everything that school is about. The learning that takes place within the school is the singular most important thing that occurs there, and your job is to ensure that students are learning and achieving to their greatest potential. This is far too broad a matter to be addressed in a small section of a book, for many volumes have been written on this topic, but it is critical for prospective school administrators to understand that their very job rests squarely on the idea that students are continually achieving and advancing. A school leader must also embrace the fact that teaching and learning are the most critical functions in helping increase student achievement.

The Internship

"With and without data, programs are engaging in improvement efforts, and there is a notable push to increase focus on the practice dimension of the profession" (Young and Peterson 2002). On numerous occasions, stakeholders have cited the lack of connection "between what is taught in many university preparation programs and what practitioners need to be able to do in their schools and school districts" (Young and Peterson). "Many policy leaders believe that at least some of the causes of the leadership problem stem from the preparation programs that train school administrators" (Olson 2000). Olson calls for a blend between coursework and on-the-job training, a provision for support, and a combination of knowledge and management training (Olson).

Teresa Gray had firsthand experience in a principal internship role and states "learning is best when it is hands-on. One can read and study all the books and journals available, but the ultimate test comes when the individual is actually in the trenches doing what must be done." Gray discusses the importance of a successful internship position as part of the final requirement for the completion of a degree in school administration. According to Gray, she "was challenged to put into practice" what she had learned in the master's program. The opportunity allowed her "to combine my research and reading, as well as the knowledge of the professors at the University of North Carolina at Charlotte, with everyday life in a public school" (Gray 2001).

In support of the need for principal internship models, Theodore B. Creighton writes, "I can think of no other profession that does not value or provide opportunities for new professionals to practice" (Creighton 2002). As examples of professions that offer practice, Creighton lists the medical profession, the legal profession, musicians, dancers, the New York Knicks, pilots, and astronauts as having "practice fields" (Creighton). The article written by Creighton refers to a part-time internship scenario; however, it enforces the need for aspiring principals to have a "safe-failing space to enhance learning" (Creighton 2002).

The Challenge

Educational leadership must be reshaped in order to raise the level of expertise. Leadership must be based on a vision firmly grounded in the knowledge and understanding of the practice of teaching and learning, The ISLLC and ELCC standards set a model of established practices for licensure in school administration.

This licensure, is official permission to practice, and certification is recognition by your peers that you do your job well. In order for preparation programs to be meaningful, they must upgrade the level of the profession, reflect the central mission of success for all students, and inform performance-based systems of assessment and evaluations for school leaders. ELCC Standard 7, the internship, brings university practices to life for the aspiring principal.

Components Necessary to a Successful Internship

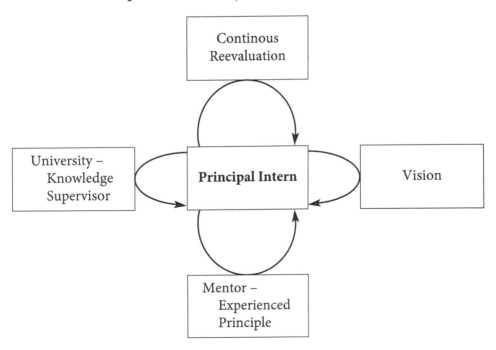

Suggested Readings

Martin, G., W. Wright W, A. Danzig, R. Flanary, and F. Brown. 2005. *School Leader Internship: Developing, Monitoring, and Evaluating Your Leadership Experience,* Second Edition. Larchmont, NY: Eye On Education.

Matthews, L., and Gary Crow. 2003. *Being and Becoming a Principal.* Boston: Pearson Learning.

Whitaker, T. 2002. *What Great Principals Do Differently.* Larchmont, NY: Eye On Education.

Suggested Activities

Questions for Discussion

1. Explore the internship requirement and the reason for adding it to the ELCC Standards.

2. Discuss the impact of the ISLLC standards on the principal's role in leadership.

3. Create a list of positive attributes for the internship component to educational leadership.

4. Discuss any perceived drawbacks of the principal internship model.

5. Explore ways to collect data to support the need for internship experiences. Devise surveys used to collect relevant data.

MAJOR CLASS ACTIVITY

Revisit the case study "Zero Tolerance" after you have experienced the internships or observations from the perspective of the principle. Has your position changed? Why or why not?

Zero Tolerance

by
Stanley A. Schainker, University of North Carolina at
Chapel Hill (with permission)

Jackie Lloyd, the first-year African-American assistant principal at the thousand-student Hilltop Middle School, has always believed that a zero tolerance policy for fighting made sense. Now she isn't so sure. Hilltop has a long-standing policy that any student involved in a fight is automatically suspended for ten school days. Late yesterday afternoon Billy Wilson, an African-American eighth grader, came into her office and told her a group of black students had been hassling him for taking school seriously and trying "to show us all up" by getting good grades. He also reported that this same group threatened him "if he didn't stop playing the Man's game." Ms. Lloyd requested the names of the students involved, and Billy reluctantly supplied them. She told him not to worry because she would take care of everything the next morning and he would be protected while at school.

The following morning she instructed the dean of students to investigate Billy's concern. She also intended to caution Billy to stay away from any place in school that would bring him into contact with the group and to alert the teachers that there could be trouble. Unfortunately, she was unable to follow through on her plans, because another emergency took her attention for the entire morning.

At lunchtime, a fight broke out in the cafeteria between Billy and four of the boys from the group he had identified. At the time there were no teachers present in the cafeteria, even though three teachers had been assigned to that monitoring assignment. Witnesses confirmed that Billy told the other boys he did not want any trouble and had fought them only after he had been pushed, kicked, and hit at least twice by the instigators. The fight was eventually stopped by the security guard with help from two teachers who escorted all five youngsters to the office.

When Ms. Lloyd talked with Billy, he tearfully asked why she had not taken care of everything and protected him as she had promised. Feeling quite guilty, she tried to explain her hectic morning, but was not successful in convincing Billy. Then she informed him she would have to suspend him for ten days for fighting because that was the automatic consequence for any fight. Incredulous, Billy argued, "In the real world people get off all the time if they kill someone in self-defense when attacked. You mean in school, if you're attacked and try to defend yourself, you get the same punishment as the attackers? That doesn't make sense! It's stupid and unfair! Do you really think I'm as guilty as the other four guys? You know I'm not. I tried to handle this the right way by coming to you, and now you're going to punish me!"

The other four boys all admitted to Lloyd that they started the fight. She then went to the principal and explained the entire case to him, and requested leeway in the suspension decision. The principal responded, "C'mon, Jackie. Don't be such a bleeding heart. You know we have a zero-tolerance policy. Billy was fighting, so he gets suspended for ten days. It's as simple as that. If he is not suspended, we undermine the whole policy and tell all the students that they can get away with fighting. This will result in chaos. Suspend him and forget about it. He'll get over it."

But Jackie Lloyd could not forget about it. Poor Jackie. Poor Billy. Poor school.

Review Session for Chapters 5–7

As promised, we have provided some additional review work for you and your class members to gain a better mastery of Standards 5, 6, and 7. We hope these activities help prepare you for any examination, but more importantly, a mastery ability of the standards to help you become a better leader with the skills to transform and change the principalship to the best it can be. Good luck!

ISLLC Standard 5

A school administrator is an educational leader who promotes the success of all students by acting with integrity, fairness, and in an ethical manner.

Scenario

Lisa is an eighth-grade student, with below-average grades, at John F. Kennedy Middle School. The student has been diagnosed with a hearing impairment and has an Individualized Education Plan (IEP) that provides her with related services. Lisa's parents believe working with a sign language instructor will improve her grades. The principal, Mr. Bohannon, asks Lisa's IEP team to assess the situation and report back to him immediately. The principal informs the parents he will report back to them as soon as possible.

Response

After research and observation, the IEP team determines that a sign language instructor will benefit Lisa and therefore should be a related service. The team explains to Mr Bohannon that the school district uses two sign language instructors to work with hearing-impaired children. The team recommends having Lisa meet weekly with the teacher. After a month, the team will reevaluate to decide if further action must be taken. Satisfied, the principal notifies Lisa's parents of the team's findings and the plan for action.

Was the response reasonable? Why or why not?

Explanation

The IEP team and principal have utilized knowledge, dispositions, and performances from ISLLC Standard 5 to ensure that the student is treated with integrity, fairness, and in an ethical manner. Using professional ethics and values for a diverse school community, Mr. Bohannon has helped create a caring school environment that supports every child's right to a free, quality education. Lunenburg and Ornstein (2000) contend that shared decision making enhances the quality of information and yields a better decision. The principal and the IEP team used laws, procedures, and sound judgment to treat the student fairly and ethically.

Do you agree? Why or why not?

ISLLC Standard 6

A school administrator is an educational leader who promotes the success of all students by understanding, responding to, and influencing the larger political, social, economic, legal, and cultural context.

Scenario

The city of Hopeville has a large budget deficit. The county commissioners are proposing to cut the education budget by $17 million. The money taken from the budget will hinder students' learning because it severely limits resources, supplies, and necessary materials appropriated to the education budget. Concerned teachers at Susan B. Anthony High School convene a meeting with the school administration to explore options. The school administration and teachers decide to use ISLLC Standard 6 to understand, respond to, and influence the larger context.

Response

The concerned educators will attend the next county commissioners meeting. Before the meeting, staff members conduct research on the negative effects of the budget cuts on students' learning. The educators have students write letters imploring the commissioners not to cut the education budget. The school also sends a letter home explaining the proposed budget reductions and asks parents to be present at the meeting.

Was the response reasonable? Why or why not?

Explanation

The school community has utilized knowledge, dispositions, and performances from ISLLC Standard 6 to promote the success of all students by understanding, responding to, and influencing the larger context of the school. Understanding that political systems greatly impact schools, the school community is communicating with and actively participating in the policy-making process. The dialogue between the educators and county commissioners ensures that the lines of communication are open and that policy is shaped to provide quality education to all students. Thomson (1992) says "school leaders must understand the necessity of adequate funds for public education, and they must convince the general public and local, state, and national legislators of the wisdom of supporting public education" (p. 13). The response to Scenario 6 demonstrates how a school administrator can promote the success of all students by understanding, responding to, and influencing the larger context of schools.

Do you agree? Why or why not?

ELCC Standard 5 (Standard 5.0)

Candidates who complete the program are educational leaders who have the knowledge and ability to promote the success of all students by acting with integrity, fairness, and in an ethical manner.

Why ELCC Standard 5 Is Necessary

The United States is a melting pot of individuals. Schools reflect the melting pot by teaching an extremely diverse student population. If children are to succeed, they must feel safe and secure while in school. One way to make students feel safe and secure is to respect their differences and treat them with integrity. All state constitutions have safeguards in place to ensure that all students are treated ethically. However, it should not take state constitutions to make principals aware that fairness, integrity, and sound ethics are necessary to educate all children.

Do you agree? Why or why not?

> *Candidates who complete the program are educational leaders who have the knowledge and ability to promote the success of all students by understanding, responding to, and influencing the larger political, social, economic, legal, and cultural context.*

Why ELCC Standard 6 Is Necessary

Schools do not operate with autonomy. They receive resources from local, state, and federal governments. Societal beliefs, fears, and pressures also influence schools. For example, curricula greatly changed after Sputnik as well as during the civil rights movement. Thomson (1992) believes that principals need an understanding of policy making and of politics, and must know how to use them to resolve educational issues and acquire support to solve problems. If schools are to operate effectively and promote students' growth and development, principals must be able to utilize and work with laws, governments, communities, professional organizations, and national associations.

Do you agree? Why or why not?

> *The internship provides significant opportunities for candidates to synthesize and apply the knowledge and practice and develop the skills identified in Standards 1 through 6 through substantial, sustained, Standards-based work in real settings, planned and guided cooperatively by the institution and school district personnel for graduate credit.*

Why ELCC Standard 7 Is Necessary

It is axiomatic that theory, knowledge, and concepts be put into practice. Only through real-world experience will MSA students learn about the intricacies associated with being a school leader. During the internship, students accept responsibilities for their actions, develop necessary communication skills, understand the larger context schools operate in, facilitate students' learning, form skills essential to fostering a positive school climate, see the great diversity in schools, and advance leadership skills.

Do you agree? Why or why not?

References

Achilles, Charles M., Jeremy D. Finn, and Helen Pate-Bain. 2002, February. Measuring class size: Let me count the ways. *Educational Leadership 59*(5), 24–26.

Administrators weigh in on what's needed to fix nation's schools. 2004, April. *Curriculum Review 43*(8), 8.

Angelides, P., and M. Ainscow. 2000. Making sense of the role of culture in school improvement. *School Effectiveness and School Improvement. 11*, 145-163.

Arsenio, W. F., S. Cooperman, and A. Lover. 2000. Affective predictors of preschoolers' aggression and peer acceptance direct and indirect effects. *Developmental Psychology 36*(4), 438–448.

Astor, R. A., H. A. Meyer, and R. O. Pitner. 2001. Elementary and middle school students' perceptions of violence-prone school subcontexts. *The Elementary School Journal 101*(5), 511–530.

Banks, J. A. and C.A.M. Banks. (Eds.). 2006. (5th Ed. 2004; 4th Ed. 2001; 3rd Ed. 1997; 2nd Ed. 1993; 1st Ed. 1989). Multicultural Education: Issues and Perspectives. 6th. Ed. New York: John Wiley.

Banks, J. A. and C.A.M. Banks. (Eds.). 2006. (5th Ed. 2004; 4th Ed. 2001; 3rd Ed. 1997; 2nd Ed. 1993; 1st Ed. 1989). *Multicultural Education: Issues and Perspectives.* 6th. Ed. New York: John Wiley.

Barbour, C., and N. Barbour. 1997. *Families, schools, and communities: building partnerships for education.* Upper Saddle River, NJ: Prentice Hall.

Barbour, C., N. Barbour, and P. Scully. 1995. *Families, schools, communities: building partnerships for educating children.* Upper Saddle River, NJ: Prentice Hall, Pg. 101.

Barclay, K. and E. Boone. 1995. *Building a three-way partnership: the leader's role in linking school, parents, and community* (Scholastic Leadership Policy Research) Scholastic Professional Book Division.

Barth, R. S. (ed.). 1990. *Improving Schools from Within*. San Francisco: Jossey-Bass.

Beckhard, W., and W. Pritchard. 1992. Changing the Essence: The Art of Creating and Leading Fundamental Change in Organizations. San Francisco: Jossey-Bass.

Bennett, J. 2000. National educational technology standards: Raising the bar by degrees. Multimedia Schools, 7(3), 16-18.

Bloch, M., and R. Tabachnick. 1994. Improving parent involvement as school reform: Rhetoric or reality? In K. Borman and N. Greenman (Eds.), Changing American education: Recapturing the past or inventing the future? 261-293. Albany: State University of New York Press.

Bloom, G., and M. Krovetz. 2001, January. A step into the principalship. *Leadership 30*(3), 12.

Blue, D. 2000. Safety by design. *Principal Leadership 1*(1), 44–47.

Borman, K. M., and W. T. Pink. 1994. *Community involvement and staff development in school improvement.* Changing Schools: Recapturing the Past or Inventing the Future? Edited by Kathryn Borman and Nancy Greenman. Albany, NY: SUNY Press.

Bracey, G. W. 2001. The condition of public education. *Phi Delta Kappan 83*(2), 157–169.

Brassard, M. 1995. *The Team Memory Jogger.* Salem: Goal QPC.

Brickell, H. M. 1964. State organization for educational change: A case study and a proposal. In M. Miles (ed), *Innovation in Education,* New York: Teachers College Press, 493–533.

Brock, B. L., and M. L. Grady. 2004. *Launching your first principalship.* Thousand Oaks, CA: Corwin Press.

Brost, P. 2000. Shared decision-making for better schools. *Principal Leadership 1*(3), 58–63.

Burns, M. K. 2002, September. Comprehensive system of assessment to intervention using curriculum-based assessments. *Intervention in School and Clinic 38*(1), 8–13.

Chase, B. 1998. Teaching right from wrong (president's viewpoint). *NEA Today 16*(7), 2(1).

Chung, K. S. (1970). ED042259 - teacher-centered management style of public school principals and job satisfaction of teachers. Retrieved January 13, 2007, from ERIC Database Web site: http://eric.ed.gov/ERICWebPortal/Home.portal?_nfpb=true&_pageLabel=RecordDetails&ERICExtSearch_SearchValue_0=ED042259&ERICExtSearch_SearchType_0=eric_accno&objectId=0900000b800c4c1b.

Cohn-Vargas, B., and K. Grose. 1998. A partnership for literacy. *Educational Leadership. 55*, 45-48.

Collinson, V. 2001. Intellectual, social, and moral development: Why technology cannot replace teachers. *High School Journal 85*(1), 35.

Copland, M. 2001, March. The myth of the superprincipal. *Phi Delta Kappan, 82*(7), 528.

Council of Chief State School Officers. 1996. *Interstate School Leaders Licensure Consortium: Standards for School Leaders.* Washington, DC: Author.

Covey, S. R. 1991. *Principle centered leadership.* New York, NY: Simon and Schuster.

Covey, S. R. 1994. *First Things First.* New York: Fireside.

Covey, S. R. 2004. *The 8th habit: from effectiveness to greatness.* New York, NY: Free Press.

Crawford, S. A. G. M., T. Hatten, D. Docheff, L. E. Lynch, S. Foy, A. Gillentine, et al. 2001. Can physical educators do more to teach ethical behavior in sports? *The Journal of Physical Education, Recreation and Dance 72*(5), 12.

Creighton, T. B. (2001). *Schools and Data: The Educator's Guide for Using Data to Improve Decision Making.* Thousand Oaks, CA: Corwin Press, Inc.

Creighton, T. B. 2002. Toward a leadership practice field: An antidote to an ailing internship experience. *The AASA Professor 25*(3), 3–9.

Davis, S., L. Darling-Hammond, M. LaPointe, and D. Meyerson. 2005. *School Leadership Study: Developing Successful Principals.* Stanford, CT: Stanford Educational Leadership Institute.

Delgado-Gaitan, Concha (editor). 1990. *Literacy for empowerment: The role of parents in their children's education.* New York: Falmer.

Donaldson, C. 2001. Something you taught me. *Reclaiming Children and Youth 10*(1), 61.

Doyle, M., and D. A. Rice. 2002. Model for instructional leadership. *Principal Leadership 3*(3), 49–52.

Duigan, P. 2005. Retrieved August 16, 2005, from e-Lead.org.

Edgar, E, N. Day-Vines, and J. M. Patton. 2002, July/August. Democratic dispositions and cultural competency. *Remedial and Special Education 23*(4), 231–242.

Ellsworth, J. B. 2000. A survey of educational change models. *ERIC Digest,* Retrieved November 16, 2006, from http://eric.ed.gov/ERICDocs/data/ericdocs2/content_storage_01/0000000b/80/2a/31/0b.pdf

Elmore, R.F., P.L. Peterson, and S.J. McCarthy. 1996. Restructuring in the classroom: Teaching, learning, and school organization. San Francisco: Jossey-Bass.

Epstein, J. L. 1995. School/family/community partnerships: caring for the children we share. *Phi Delta Kappan. 76.*

Epstein, J. L. 2001. School, family, and community partnerships: Preparing educators and improving schools. Boulder, CO: Westview Press.

Espelage, D. L., K. Bosworth, and T. R. Simon. 2000. Examining the social context of bullying behaviors in early adolescence. *Journal of Counseling and Development 78*(3), 326–334.

Fan, X., and M. Chen. 2001. Parental involvement and students' academic achievement: a meta-analysis. *Educational Psychology Review. 13*, 1-22.

Fesmire, S. 2001. Ecological humanism a moral image for our emotive cult. *The Humanist 61*(1), 27.

Fowler, F. C. 2000. *Policy Studies for Educational Leaders: An Introduction.* Upper Saddle River, NJ: Merrill/Prentice Hall.

Fullan, M. G. 1999. *Change forces: the sequel.* Oxford, UK: Routledge.

Gips, M. A. 2002. A good resource for schools? *Security Management 46*(1), 18–19.

Gray, T. I. 2001. Principal internships. *Phi Delta Kappan 82*(9), 663.

Greenfield, W. 1987. *Instructional leadership: concepts, issues, and controversies.* Massachusetts: Allyn & Bacon.

Griffiths, D. E. 1963. The elementary school principal and change in the school system. *Theory Into Practice 2*, 278–284.

Groff, F. 2001, October/November. Who will lead? The principal shortage. *State Legislatures, 27*(9), 16.

Grossman, D. 2000/2001. We are training our kids to kill. *Annual Editions: Deviant Behavior,* 39–44.

Gutierrez, R. 2001. Rekindling concerns over moral politics in the classroom. *The Social Studies 92*(3), 113.

Hansen, J. M., and J. Childs. 1998. Creating a school where people like to be. (Realizing a positive school climate.) *Educational Leadership 56*(1), 14.

Hargrove, E., and J. Glidewell. 2001. *Impossible jobs in public management.* Lawrence, KS: University Press of Kansas.

Hatch, T. 1998. How community action contributes to achievement. *Educational Leadership, 55*, 16-19.

Hazler, R. J. (1994). Bullying breeds violence. You can stop it! *Learning 22*(6), 38–41.

Henderson, J. G., and R. D. Hawthorne. 2000. *Transformative Curriculum Leadership* 2nd ed., Upper Saddle River, NJ: Prentice Hall.

Hinebauch, S. 2002, Summer. Nurturing the emerging independent adolescent. *Independent School 61*(4), 18–23.

Hoachlander G., A. C. Sikora, and L. Horn. 2003. Community college students: Goals, academic preparation, and outcomes. (NCES Report No. 2003-164). Washington, DC: National Center for Education Statistics.

Honeyman, D. S. 1994. Finances and the problems of America's school buildings. *Clearing House 68*(2), 95–98.

Hord, S. M. 1992. Facilitative leadership: the imperative for change. *SEDL,* Retrieved November 16, 2006, from http://www.sedl.org/change/facilitate/

Howe, M. L., and R. Townsend. 2000. The principal as political leader. *The High School Magazine 7*(6), 10–16.

Hoy, W. K., and S. R. Sweetland. 2001. Designing better schools: The meaning and measure of enabling school structures. *Educational Administration Quarterly 37*(3), 296–321.

Huesmann, L. R., and N. G. Guerra. 1997. Children's normative beliefs about aggression and aggressive behavior. *Journal of Personality and Social Psychology 72*(2), 408–419.

Huffman, H. A. 1993. Character education without turmoil. *Educational Leadership 51*(3), 24–26.

Hunter, J. D. 2000. Leading children beyond good and evil. *First Things: A Monthly Journal of Religion and Public Life 5*, 36.

ISTE. 2002. Educational Technology Standards. Retrieved January 12, 2007, from International Society for Technology in Education Web site: http://cnets.iste.org/administrators/a_stands.html.

Institute of Educational Leadership (2000). Leadership for student learning: Reinventing the principalship [electronic version]. Retrieved February 8, 2002, from www.iel.org/programs/21st/reports/principal.pdf.

Interstate School Leaders Licensure Consortium. (1996). *ISLLC Standards for School Leaders.* Retrieved February 5, 2003, from Council of Chief State School Officers Web Site: www.ccsso.org/islcc.html.

Johnson, D. W. 1970. *The Social Psychology of Education.* San Francisco: Holt, Rinehart, and Winston.

Joyce, B., D. Hopkins, and E. Calhoun. 2006. *The new structure of school improvement: inquiring schools and achieving students.* Berkshire, UK: Open University Press.

Joyce, B., M. Weil, and E. Y. Calhoun. 2000. *Models of Teaching,* 6th ed. Needham Heights, MA: Allyn and Bacon.

Joyce, S. 2000. Pencils, backpacks, and lawsuits. *The High School Magazine 7*(6), 17–19.

Kennedy, M. 2002. Balancing security and learning. *American School and University 74*(6), 8–11.

Kerrins, J., T. Johnstone, and K. Cushing. 2001, May. Take this job and fill it. *Leadership 30*(5), 20.

King, D. (2002). The changing shape of leadership [electronic version]. *Association for Supervision and Curriculum Development 59*(8), 61–63.

Klein, J. 1993. How about a swift kick? *Newsweek 122*(4), 30.

Kohn, A. 1998. *What to Look for in a Classroom . . . and Other Essays.* San Francisco: Jossey-Bass.

Ladd, G. W., and S. M. Profilet. 1996. The child behavior scale: A teacher-report measure of young children's aggressive, withdrawn, and prosocial behaviors. *Developmental Psychology 32*(6), 1008–1024.

Lake, V. E. 2001. Linking literacy and moral education in the primary classroom (teaching ideas). *The Reading Teacher 55*(2), 125–129.

Lashway, L. (1997). Visionary Leadership. (Report No. 110). Eugene, OR. (ERIC Documentation Reproduction Service No. ED 402643)

Lashway, L. 2000. Who's in charge? The accountability challenge. *Principal Leadership 1*(3), 8–13.

Lauder, A. 2000. The new look in principal preparation programs. *National Association of Secondary School Principals 84*(617), 23–28.

Lehr, Fran. "Revision in the Writing Process". Reading and Communication Skills. 1 Jan. 1995. ERIC Digests.26Sept2001.<http://ehostvgw19.epnet/delivery.asp…hr&startHitNum=1&rlStartHit=1&delType=FT>

Lewin, K., R. Lippitt, and R. K. White. 1939. Patterns of aggressive behavior in experimentally created "social climates." *Journal of Social Psychology 10*, 271–299.

Lickona, T. 1993. The return of character education (the Character Education Partnership, Inc.). *Educational Leadership 51*(3), 6–11.

Lochman, J. E., J. D. Coie, M. K. Underwood, and R. Terry. 1993. Effectiveness of a social relations intervention program for aggressive and nonaggressive, rejected children. *Journal of Consulting and Clinical Psychology 61*(6), 1053–1058.

Loeb, M., and S. Kindel. 1999. *Leadership for Dummies*. Forest City, CA: IDG Books Worldwise.

Lunenburg, F. C., and A. C. Ornstein. 2000. *Educational Administration: Concepts and Practices,* 3rd ed. Belmont, CA: Wadswoth/Thomson.

Lyons, J. 2002. Major responsibilities of principals. Unpublished table, University of North Carolina at Charlotte.

Maier, N. R. F., and G. C. Verser. 1982. *Psychology in Industrial Organizations,* 5th ed. Boston: Houghton-Mifflin.

Maslow, A. H. (ed.). 1973. *Dominance, Self-esteem, Self-actualization: Germinal Papers of A. H. Maslow.* Monterey, CA: Brooks/Cole.

Matthews, L. J., and G. M. Crow. 2003. *Being and Becoming a Principal: Role Conceptions for Contemporary Principals and Assistant Principals.* Boston: Allyn and Bacon.

Mattocks, T. C., and D. D. Drake. (2001). The preparation of visionary leaders for practitioner roles: A challenge for graduate programs in educational administration and school organizations [electronic version]. Retrieved February 5, 2002, from www.aasa.org/publications/tap/Winter_2001.pdf+preparation+of+visionary+leaders+%22Mattocks%22&hl=en&ie=UTF-8.

McAdams, R. P. 1997, October. A systems approach to school reform. *Phi Delta Kappan 79*(2), 138–142.

McCall, J. R. 1994. *The Provident Principal,* 2nd ed. Chapel Hill, NC: Principals' Executive Program.

McCay, E. (2001). The learning needs of principals. *Association for Supervision and Curriculum Development 58*(8), 75–78.

Mendez-Morse, S. 1992. Leadership characteristics that facilitate school change. Southwest Educational Development Laboratory. Retrieved February18, 2004, from www.sedl.org/change/leadership/character/html.

Miller, A. W. 2001. Finding time and support for instructional leadership. *Principal Leadership 12*(4), 29–33.

Mintzberg, H. 1989. *Mintzberg on Management.* New York: The Free Press.

Morgan, G. 1997. *Images of Organizations, 2nd ed.* Thousand Oaks, CA: Sage.

Murphy, J. 1998. Preparation for the school principalship: The United States' story. *School Leadership and Management 18*(3), 1–12.

Murphy, J. 2002. How the ISLLC standards are reshaping the principalship. *Principal 82*(1), 22–26.

Murphy, J. and K. S. Louis. 1994. *Reshaping the Principalship: Insights from Transformational Efforts.* Thousand Oaks, CA: Sage.

Murphy, J., J. Yff, and N. Shipman. 2000. Implementation of the Interstate School Leaders Licensure Consortium standards [electronic version]. *Leadership in Education 3*(1), 17–39.

NCREL. 2002. Critical issue: using technology to improve student achievement. Retrieved November 16, 2006, Web site: http://www.ncrel.org/sdrs/areas/issues/methods/technlgy/te800.htm#researchresult

Nanus, B. (1989). *The Leader's Edge.* Chicago: Contemporary Books.

Nanus, B. (1992). *Visionary Leadership.* San Francisco: Jossey-Bass.

National Association of Elementary School Principals. 2003. *Leading Learning Communities: NAESP Standards for What Principals Should Know and Be Able to Do.* Alexandria VA National Association of Elementary School Principals.

National Association of Secondary School Principals. 1996. *Breaking Ranks: Changing an American Institution.* Reston, VA: Author.

National Center for Education Statistics. 2001, May. Internet access in U.S. public schools and classrooms: 1994-2000. Retrieved January 12, 2007, from IES: National Center for Education Statistics Web site: http://nces.ed.gov/pubsearch/pubsinfo.asp?pubid=2001071

National Partnership for Excellence and Accountability in Teaching (NPEAT). 1999. Characteristics of effective professional development. Retrieved July 20, 2006 from http://ed-web3.educ.msu.edu/npeat/.

National Policy Board for Educational Administration (2002). Instructions to implement standards for advanced programs in educational leadership: For principals, superintendents, curriculum directors, and supervisors. Retrieved February 5, 2002, from www.ncate.org/standard/new%20program%20standards/elcc.pdf.

Neave, Henry. 1990. *The Deming Dimension* (Hutchinson, London).

Newcomb, A. F., W. M. Bukowski, and L. Pattee. 1993. Children's peer relations: A meta-analytic review of popular, rejected, neglected, controversial, and average sociometric status. *Psychological Bulletin 113*(1), 99–128.

Nieto, S. 2000. Placing equity front and center: some thoughts on transforming teacher education for a new century. *Journal of Teacher Education. 51,* 180-187.

Norris, C. J., B. G. Barnett, M. R. Basom, and D. M. Yerkes. 2002. *Developing Educational Leaders: A Working Model: The Learning Community in Action.* New York: Teachers College Press.

North Carolina Department of Juvenile Justice and Delinquency Prevention. (n.d.). 1999 sourcebook of preventing school violence. Retrieved June 22, 2002, from www.ncsu.edu/cpsv/cpsvrroom.htm.

Odden, A. 2001. The new school finance. *Phi Delta Kappan 83*(1), 85–91.

Odden, A., and S. Archibald. 2000. The possibilities of resource reallocation. *Principal Leadership 1*(3), 26–32.

Olson, L. 2000, January 19. New thinking on what makes a leader. Retrieved January 27, 2003, from www.edweek.org/ew/ew_printstory.cfm?slug=19leade.h19.

Oswald, L. J. 1995. *Priority on Learning: Efficient Use of Resources.* (Report No. OERI.RR93002006). Eugene, OR: University of Oregon. (ERIC Document Reproduction Service No. ED435395).

Owens, R.G. 1995. *Organizational behavior in education* (5th ed.). Boston: Allyn and Bacon.

O'Toole, M. E. (n.d.). *The School Shooter: A Threat Assessment Perspective.* Quantico, VA: Federal Bureau of Investigation.

Palmer, P. 1998. *The courage to teach.* San Francisco: Jossey-Bass.

Pastor, P. 2002. School discipline and the character of our schools. *Phi Delta Kappan 83*(9), 658–661.

Patti, J., and J. Tobin. 2001. Leading the way: Reflections on creating peaceable schools. *Reclaiming Children and Youth 10*(1), 41–46.

Pawlas, G. 1995. *The Administrator's Guide to School Community Relations.* New York: Eye on Education.

Peterson, K., and C. Kelley. 2001, January. Transforming school leadership. *Leadership 30*(3), 8.

Phlegar, J. M., and N. Hurley. 1999. Designing job embedded professional learning: the authentic task approach. *Learning Innovations.* 1-15.

Picus, L. O. 2000. *How Schools Allocate and Use Their Resources.* (Report No. EDO-EA-00). Eugene, OR: University of Oregon. (ERIC Document Reproduction Service No. ED452578).

Piquero, N. L., and S. S. Simpson. 2002. Low self-control, organizational theory, and corporate crime. *Law and Society Review 36*(3), 509–548.

Plato. *The Republic* (B. Jowett, MA, trans.). New York: Vintage Books.

Preskill, H. S., and R. T. Torres. 1998. *Evaluative inquiry for learning in organizations.* Thousand Oaks, CA: Sage Publications.

Public Education Network. 2001. Strategic planning. Retrieved August 29, 2001, from www.publiceducation.org/resources/od1.htm.

Purcell, J., N. Kinnie, and S. Hutchinson. 2003, May. Open minded. *People Management 9*(10).

Quality counts. (2002). Resources: Equity. *Education Week 21*(17), 88, 89.

Queen, J. A., and R. F. Algozzine, 2007a. *The Responsible Discipline Handbook.* Charlotte: The Writer's Edge.

Quinn, T. 2002. The inevitable school crisis: Are you ready? *Principal 81*(5), 6–8.

Raywid, M. A. 2002, February. Accountability: What's worth measuring? *Phi Delta Kappan 83*(6), 433–436.

Reeve, E. M. 2002, October. Translating standards for technological literacy into curriculum. *Technology Teacher 62*(2), 33–36.

Robenstine, C. 2000. School choice and administrators: will principals become marketers? *The Clearing House. 74*, 95-98.

Rogenski, K. 1996. Control your staff meetings. *Thrust for Educational Leadership 26*(2), 14–17.

Rooney, J. 2000. Survival skills for the new principal. *Educational Leadership*, 58 (1), 77-78.

Rose, L., and A. Gallup. 2005. 36th Phi Delta Kappan Gallup poll of public attitudes toward the public schools. *Phi Delta Kappan 86*, 41–58.

Royal, M. A., and R. J. Rossi. 1997, March. Schools as communities. *ERIC Digest 111*.

Sammon, G., and M. Becton. 2001. Principles of partnerships. *Principal Leadership 1*(8), 32–35.

Sanders, M. G. 2001.The role of "community" in comprehensive school, family, and community partnership programs. *The Elementary School Journal. 102*, 19–34.

Sanoff, H., C. Pasalar, and M. Hashas. 2001. *School building assessment methods*. National Clearinghouse for Educational Facilities Washington.

Schargel, F. P. 1994. *Transforming Education through Total Quality Management*. Princeton: Eye on Education.

Schlechty, Phillip C. 1990. *Schools for the Twenty-first Century: Leadership Imperatives for Educational Reform*. San Francisco: Jossey-Bass, 1990.

Schneider, M. 2002. *Public school facilities and teaching*. New York, NY: Ford Foundation.

Senge, P., N. Cambron-McCabe, T. Lucas, B. Smith, J. Dutton, and A. Kleiner. 2000. *Schools That Learn: A Fifth Discipline Fieldbook for Educators, Parents, and Everyone Who Cares about Education*. New York: Doubleday.

Sergiovanni, T. J. 1990. *Value-Added Leadership: How to get Extraordinary Performance in Schools*. Orlando, FL: Harcourt, Brace, Jovanovich.

Sergiovanni, T. J. 1992. *Moral Leadership: Getting to the Heart of School Improvement*. San Francisco: Jossey-Bass.

Shipman, N. J. 2003. *Speech to principal fellows group*. UNC Charlotte: unpublished.

Sizer, T. R., and N. F. Sizer. 1999. Grappling. *Phi Delta Kappan 81*(3), 184.

Slosson, J. 2000. Taming the budget process. *Principal Leadership 1*(3), 54–57.

Slowinski, J. 2000. Becoming a technology savvy administrator. *ERIC Digest 135*.

Snow, A. L. 2003. *Practical Advice for Principals*. Lanham, MD: Scarecrow Press.

Solomon, R. N. (Ed.). (2000). *Creating an appetite for change* Washington D.C.: Policy Studies Associates, Inc.

Sparks, Dennis. 2002. *Designing Powerful Professional Development for Teachers and Principals*. Oxford, OH: National Staff Development Council.

Spence, D. (Ed.). *Southern Regional Education Board*. 2006. *Challenge to Lead: The Momentum Continues* Atlanta, GA.

Stattin, H., and D. Magnusson. 1989. The role of early aggressive behavior in the frequency, seriousness, and types of later crime. *Journal of Consulting and Clinical Psychology 57*(6), 710–718.

Taylor, R. 2002. Shaping the culture of learning communities. *Principal Leadership 3*(4), 42–45.

Thomson, S. D. 1992. *School Leadership: A Blueprint for Change*. Newbury Park, CA: Corwin Press.

Tirozzi, G., and V. Ferrandino. 2001, January 31. How do you reinvent a principal? [electronic version]. *Education Week*. Retrieved March 11, 2006, from www.naesp.org/ContentLoad.do?contentId=902.

Toffler, A., and H. Toffler. 1995. *Creating a new civilization*. Atlanta: Turner Publishing.

Trump, K. S. 2002. Be prepared, not scared. *Principal 81*(5), 10–14.

Tyack, D., and L. Cuban. 1995. *Tinkering Toward Utopia: A Century of Public School Reform*. Cambridge, MA: Harvard University Press.

US Department of Education. 2004. Innovations in education: successful charter schools. Retrieved November 16, 2006, from US Charter Schools Web site: http://www.ed.gov/admins/comm/choice/charter/

US Department of Labor. 2004. Education administrators. Retrieved January 12, 2007, from Bureau of Labor Statistics Web site: http://stats.bls.gov/oco/pdf/ocos007.pdf.

Ubben, Gerald, L. Hughes, and C. Norris. 2001. *The Principal: Creative a Leadership for Effective Schools*. Needham Heights, MA: Allyn & Bacon.

United States Bureau of Labor Statistics - USBLS. 2002. *Occupational outlook handbook*. Washington, DC.

Vincent, A., and M. Meche. (2001). Use of ethical dilemmas to contribute to the knowledge and behavior of high school students. *High School Journal 84(4)*, 50.

Vossekuil, B., M. Reddy, and R. Fein. 2000. *Safe school initiative: An interim report on* Administrator shortage worsens. 2002, January. *Curriculum Review 41*(5), 3.

Wallace, R. C. (1996). From vision to practice. Thousand Oaks: CA Sage Publications Company.

Yanitski, N. W. 1997. *Site-Based Management: Its Impact on School Decision-Making*. Unpublished Doctoral Dissertation, University of Alberta, Edmonton, AB.

Young, M. D., and G. J. Peterson. 2002. Enabling substantive reform in the preparation of school leaders. *Education Leadership Review 3*(1), 1–15.

Index

Bush, George W., 141
business-sponsored scholarships, 103

C

Calhoun, E., 32, 117
cardiopulmonary resuscitation (CPR)
    training, 73
*Celebration of Neurons, A: An Educator's Guide
    to the Human Brain* (Sylwester), 28
Center for the Prevention of School
    Violence, 71, 73
change
    attitudes toward, 34
    capacity for, 148
    culture for, 10
    leader of, 17
    phases of, 34
    principals and, 146–48
    resistance to, 146
    responding to, 138
    in school culture, 35–36
change agents, 34, 138, 146–48
change processes, 34
character education, 84
Character Education Partnership, 125
character education programs
    formal, 125
    informal, 125–26
Chase, B., 125
cheating, 128
chief financial officer (CFO), 61
Chung, K. S., 147
codes of ethics, 121–23
cognitivist theory, 29
collaboration (standard four), 87–110
    assessment of, 97–98
    broad community involvement in, 102–3
    challenge of, 108
    chapter assignment for, 109–10
    ELCC on, 87, 88, 97, 101, 118
    importance of, 95–96, 100, 102–3
    interagency, 94
    internal public in, 103–6
    ISLLC on, 87, 88, 97, 101, 115
    parents and, 90–91, 95–96, 98, 99, 100–102
    principals and, 89–90, 94–95, 97, 100, 106–7
    research on, 106
    school community relations plan for, 98–99,
        106–7
    students and, 95, 96, 100, 102–3, 105
    suggested activities for, 108–9
    teachers and, 91, 92–93, 104–5
collegial climate, 40–41

Comer, James, 102
Comer School Development Process, 102,
    106, 107
Committee on Economic Development, 68
common school movement, 157
Common School Teacher's Association, 157
communication skills, 5–8
    for articulating vision, 15
    for collaboration, 90–91, 92, 98–99, 100
    for consensus building, 8
    for interviews, 5–8
    for management, 65–67
    for negotiation, 8
    written, 5
community. *See* collaboration
community center, 92
community relations plan, 98–99, 106–7
community resources, 93–94
community surveys, 98
computers, 34
conflict management, 144–45
Connecticut School Effectiveness
    Project, 10
consensus-building skills, 8, 13–14, 143
constructivist theory, 29
continuous improvement, 9
Cooperman, S., 80
corporal punishment, 59
Covey, Stephen, 65, 70, 120, 126
CPR training, 73
Crawford, S. A., 130
Creighton, T. B., 5, 161
Crime Prevention Through Environmental
    Design (CPTED), 71, 72
crisis plan, 73
curriculum
    design of, 29–30, 49–54
    evaluation and refinement of, 29–30
    implementation of, 29–30
custodian, 104
cyber bullying, 80

D

data analysis, 4–5, 30
data collection, 4–5, 30
David A. Ellis School (Boston), 102
decentralization, 57
decision making, 95, 142–44
Deming's continuous improvement model, 9
democratic leaders, 143–44, 148
democratic values, 2
Department of Education, 34
Department of Labor, 62, 131